101 SCIENCE EXPERIMENTS
POP
for the MAD SCIENTIST
SIZZLE
in EVERY KID
BOOM!

AMY OYLER
ILLUSTRATED BY AMANDA BRACK

Castle Point Books
NEW YORK

TO KATIE AND MAIZY,
for whom the brightest sparks of curiosity
have led to a lifetime of discovery.

TO NATHAN,
whose love and support has encouraged
our inquisitive minds to bloom.

—A.O.

www.stmartins.com
www.castlepointbooks.com

The Castle Point Books trademark is owned by Castle Point Publications, LLC.
Castle Point books are published and distributed by St. Martin's Press.

Design by Katie Jennings Campbell

ISBN 978-1-250-09282-3 (trade paperback)
ISBN 978-1-250-16556-5 (e-book)

Our books may be purchased in bulk for promotional, educational,
or business use. Please contact your local bookseller or the
Macmillan Corporate and Premium Sales Department at 1-800-221-7945,
extension 5442, or by e-mail at MacmillanSpecialMarkets@macmillan.com.

First Edition: June 2017

10 9 8 7 6 5 4 3 2 1

CONTENTS

CHAPTER 1
SHINE, SPIN, SIZZLE
THE POWER OF THE SUN
4 Solar-Powered Pinwheels
6 Solar Photography
8 Build a Solar Oven
11 Build a Pinhole Solar
Eclipse Viewer
14 Building a Spectrometer

CHAPTER 2
DIG, PLANT, PLUCK
SCIENCE IN THE GARDEN
18 Autumn Leaf Mash-Up
21 May the Best Soil Win
23 Make Your Own Compost
25 Make a Leaf Skeleton
28 Color-Changing Carnations
30 Build a Water Filter with Sand
and Rocks

CHAPTER 3
STOMP, PECK, SOAR
AMAZING BUGS AND ANIMALS
34 Fossil Footprints
36 Darwin's Finches
38 The Ants Go Marching
40 Bright Lights and Buggy Nights
42 Finding Life in a Drop of Water
44 Build an Insect Hotel

CHAPTER 4
SPLISH, SPLASH, SWIRL
COOL KITCHEN EXPERIMENTS
48 Squishing Out Strawberry DNA
51 Rotten Apple Chemistry
54 Disappearing Eggshells
56 A Dish of Dancing Rainbows
58 Cabbage-Water Chemistry
60 Fabric Art with Acids and Bases
62 Liquid Rainbow Tower
64 Sinking and Floating Eggs

CHAPTER 5
NIBBLE, CHEW, CRUNCH
THE SCIENCE OF CANDY
67 Candy Chromatography
70 Inside a Gobstopper
72 Floating Candy Letters
74 Marshmallow Animals Gone Wild
76 Lightning Life Savers

CHAPTER 6
SNIP, SNIP, GLUE:
BUILDING REALISTIC BODY PARTS
79 Build a Balloon Lung
81 Make a Skeleton Hand
83 Eat Your Cake and Digest It Too
85 The Big Squeeze: Intestines
at Work
88 A Bloody-Good Heart Pump
90 Crafting the Human Heart

CHAPTER 7

SEE, SNIFF, SLURP
TEST YOUR SENSES

94   Make a Frozen Lens
96   Colorblind Taste Test
98   Sound Gun Science
100 The Ouch Sensitivity Test
102 The Scent Detective Game
104 Smell it, Don't Tell It

CHAPTER 8

GLOP, STRETCH, SPLAT
ADVENTURES IN SLIME

107 It's Alive: The Properties of Slime
109 Bouncing Polymer Putty
111 Water Bead Osmosis
113 The Science of Stickiness

CHAPTER 9

FIZZ, BUBBLE, POP
ALL THINGS FUN AND GASSY

116 Erupting Soda Geysers
118 Bubbling Wonders Lava Lamp
120 Fizzing Volcanoes
122 Color-Changing Explosions
124 Elephant Toothpaste
126 It's a Gas! The Magic of CO_2
128 Grow a Giant Carbon Snake

CHAPTER 10

RUMBLE, RUMBLE, SHAKE:
ERUPTING EARTH SCIENCE

132 Build an Underwater Volcano
135 Jello Earthquake Engineering
137 Sample the Earth's Core
139 Cookie Continents and Ocean Erosion
142 Playdoh Plate Tectonics

CHAPTER 11

SIMMER, SQUISH, STACK:
GEOLOGY AT ITS BEST

146 Molten Magma Rock Candy
149 Crystal Salt Tower
151 Metamorphic Candy Bars: The Science of the Squish
153 Seven-Layer Sedimentary Crackers
155 Grow Your Own Crystal Garden
157 Dazzling Crystal Snowflakes
159 Hair-Raising Jello Stalagmites

CHAPTER 12

PUSH, PULL, SWING:
ALL CHARGED UP ABOUT MAGNETS

162 Dancing Magnetic Slime
164 Magnetic Cereal: Where's the Iron?
166 The Magnet-Powered Pendulum
168 Recording Magnetic Fields
170 Make Your Own Bottle-Cork Compass

I Love science

CHAPTER 13
WHOOSH, SWISH, FLUTTER:
THE SCIENCE OF WEATHER
173 Snow in Summer
175 Build a Tornado Chamber
178 Frosty the Snow Can
180 Cloud in a bottle
182 Convection Currents
in the Atmosphere

CHAPTER 14
DRIP, DROP, POP:
EXPERIMENTS WITH BUBBLES
185 Whatever Floats Your Boat
187 Poking Holes and Plugging Leaks
189 Make Bubbles with Dry Ice
191 Colorful Bubble Art
193 Bouncing Bubbles

CHAPTER 15
CRACKLE, CRACKLE, ZAP
ADVENTURES IN ELECTRICITY
197 Charming Snakes with Static
Electricity
199 Electrified Aluminum Can Racing
201 The Art of Water Bending
203 Flying Tinsel Cloud
205 Make Your Own Lemon Battery
207 Make Circuits with Play-Doh

CHAPTER 16
REV, ZOOM, ROCKET
THE SCIENCE OF SPEED
211 Vortex Water Races
213 Build a Marble Run
215 Build a Water Rocket
218 Fly High with a Stomp Rocket
221 Balloon Boat Races
224 Mentos and Diet Soda Rocket Car

CHAPTER 17
CRUSH, CRUMPLE, SHRIEK
OBJECTS UNDER PRESSURE
228 Air Pressure Can Crushing
230 Water on the Rise
232 Dry-Ice Screaming Pennies
234 Pressure-Powered Submarines
236 Egg in a Bottle

CHAPTER 18
SHINE, SHIMMER, GLOW
THE MYSTERIES OF SPACE
239 Dropping Meteors on the Moon
241 Chocolate Cookie Moon Phases
244 Build a Working Telescope
246 Flashlight Constellations

An Introduction to the World of

POP SIZZLE BOOM!

Kids are natural-born scientists who see the world through a lens of curiosity and wonder. They want to get out and see the world, to dig deep in the earth and see what they can find. They want to mix ingredients and create bursts of color-changing chemical reactions. They want to engineer their own race tracks, launch their own rockets, and build their own telescopes to look to the moon and stars above. To them, the world has no limits, so they're more than willing to embark on an adventure of limitless scientific discovery.

Just as scientific curiosity spans the ages, so too do the experiments in this book. You'll find experiments fit for the youngest little explorer (they'll love "Frosty the Snow Can" in Chapter 13), and others that will ignite the fire of curiosity in the most seasoned young scientist. (What kid doesn't want to try "Grow a Giant Carbon Snake?") Allow your kids to do as much as their ages will naturally allow, to build upon their confidence as young scientists and to keep them fully engaged.

Parents are the key to making this book come to life. For that reason, the book is designed with parents' needs in mind. Most of the experiments, for example, use common household materials, or items that could easily be found at a hardware store. The instructions are easy to understand and lively art helps to fuel your child's imagination and set the tone for this exciting learning voyage. Use the time indicator on the left-hand side of the page so that you know ahead of time which experiments are right for you and your child. You don't have to be a science expert to help your child learn: that part is done for you. After each experiment, you'll find a helpful blurb that explains the science in clear terms. In some instances, a "Take it Further" section is added to help extra-curious kids (or their parents) go even deeper with their learning and exploration.

Treat this book as a guide and flip through the pages with your child to see where his or her interests take you. Follow your children's curiosity and help them get to the bottom of their own burning questions about the world around them. Your children are about to follow in the footsteps of world-famous scientists as they embark on their own thrilling adventure through the popping, sizzling, exploding wonders of science!

Happy Exploring!

AMY OYLER

blogger, scientist, mom

SHINE

CHAPTER 1

SPIN

THE POWER OF THE SUN

SIZZLE

SOLAR-POWERED PINWHEELS

Everyone loves the classic fun of a spinning pinwheel, but did you know you can make one of your own and spin it with the power of the sun? With this experiment, you'll build a tower of solar energy, and use that instead of your breath to power your very own pinwheel! All you need are some aluminum cans, a stack of books, and some paper, and you're on your way to a spinning adventure in physics!

MATERIALS NEEDED

3 aluminum cans

Can opener

Masking tape

Large paper clip

Thumbtack

Ruler

Paper

Scissors

Pencil

Stack of books

PROCEDURE

1. Remove both ends from all the aluminum cans with a can opener. Then build a tower by stacking them on top of each other and taping them into place. Use masking tape to create a seal around each can where it meets the next one in the tower.

2. Straighten the paper clip and bend it into an arch. Tape the ends to each side of the top of the aluminum can tower so that it arches across the opening in your tower.

3. Tape the thumbtack to the center of the paper clip so that the sharp end is pointing straight up.

4. Use your ruler to draw a 6" square on your piece of paper, then cut it out. Make a pinwheel by making a diagonal cut from each corner to the center of the paper, stopping about ¼" before the center.

5. Once you have made four cuts from the corners of your square, take the right side of each cut, and fold it into the center. Tape the meeting points in the center to create your pinwheel.

6. Create two 2" stacks of books in a sunny spot of your home or outside. Place the book stacks 1 ½" apart, and place your aluminum can tower on the stacks so that the can sits across the gap.

7. Balance your paper pinwheel on the point of the thumbtack. Once it's balanced, sit back and watch it spin!

WHAT'S HAPPENING?

The sun releases energy that we can see as light and feel as heat. This energy powers everything on Earth. We can harness this energy by collecting it in battery cells, and use it to power our homes. In this experiment, the aluminum cans harness the sun's energy. The heat from the sun collects at the bottom of the can. and rises to the top. As this energy moves through the can, it pushes your pinwheel, spinning it!

SOLAR PHOTOGRAPHY

You know you can take a photograph with a camera or a smartphone, but did you know you could create a photograph with the sun and a piece of paper? With solar imprint paper, you can create an image using the ultraviolet rays from the sun and create your own work of art with solar photography! All you need is some solar imprint paper (found online or in the science and education section of your local toy store), some natural materials, and a sunny day.

MATERIALS NEEDED

Solar imprint paper

Leaves, feathers, or toys

Plastic wrap (optional)

Paper towels

PROCEDURE

1. Gather natural materials that will lie flat and have interesting shapes. Leaves, feathers, and flowers work well for this activity.

2. Carefully remove one of the sheets of solar imprint paper. Create a natural mosaic with your materials by placing them to form a picture on your paper.

3. Find a sunny spot outside to place your work of art. Leave it there for 1-3 minutes. If there is a breeze, you can place a piece of clear plastic over your artwork to keep it in place.

4. After the paper has turned white, bring it inside, remove the objects, and place the paper in a shallow tray filled with water. Let it soak for about one minute.

5. Remove the paper from the tray, and set it on a paper towel. Using the paper towel, pat the paper to remove any excess water.

6. Lay the paper flat to dry. Once the paper starts to curl up on the corners, you can lay a book on top of it to keep it flat as it dries.

7. Once the paper is fully dry, you can frame your solar artwork and hang it on your wall!

WHAT'S HAPPENING?

The solar photo paper is treated with a solution of chemicals that are UV sensitive, which means they will change color when exposed to the ultraviolet rays from the sun. When you place objects on the paper, these objects prevent the UV rays from hitting the paper, which prevents it from changing color. When the solution is rinsed away, it stops the process of UV light interaction and keeps your photo from changing again.

—30

—20

—10

Build a
SOLAR OVEN

Have you ever heard the phrase, "It's as hot as an oven"? Believe it or not, the sun's heat energy actually could be used as an oven! We harness solar energy in solar panels to provide electricity and battery power, but we can harness solar energy to cook our food, too. Combining solar energy with the perfect summer snack is as easy as using some household materials, and taking advantage of a hot day. Then you'll be well on your way to summer s'mores, cooked with the power of the sun!

MATERIALS NEEDED

Pizza box

Ruler

Box cutter

Aluminum foil

Tape

Plastic wrap

Black construction paper

S'mores ingredients: graham crackers, chocolate bar, marshmallows

Wooden skewer

PROCEDURE

1. Use your ruler to draw a large square on the top of the pizza box, making sure that the square is about 2" away from the edges on all sides.

2. Use your box cutter to cut three sides out of the square, leaving the back side as the hinge. When you are finished cutting, fold the square upwards at an angle.

3. Cover the inside of the flap (facing the inside of the box) with aluminum foil. Make sure that this layer is pulled tightly around the flap and tape it to the back of the flap to secure it in place. This will be your reflector window, reflecting the sun's rays into your oven.

4. Cover the opening below your flap with plastic wrap. Make sure that the window is tightly sealed, and that there are no rips or tears in the plastic wrap. Use tape to secure the edges of the plastic wrap to the top of the pizza box.

5. Line the inside of the pizza box with aluminum foil. You'll want to reflect as much light into your oven as possible to focus the solar energy onto what you are cooking.

6. Place a marshmallow and a small piece of chocolate on a graham cracker, and put your s'more on a square of aluminum foil. Place your s'more on a piece of black construction paper and slide it inside your pizza box oven under the plastic wrap window.

7. Finally, prop up the reflector flap with the wooden skewer, angling it near 90 degrees, making sure it is reflecting the sun's rays directly down into your pizza box oven.

8. Leave your solar oven out in direct sunlight (angled so that the flap is catching the sun's direct rays) for at least 30 minutes. This works best on a hot day, with temperatures at 85 degrees Fahrenheit or greater.

WHAT'S HAPPENING?

You are capturing the sun's energy to cook your food. When you cut the flap out of the pizza box and cover it with foil, you angle the sun's rays into your oven. The foil acts as a reflector, further bouncing light and heat around your food. The plastic wrap keeps heat contained inside the box. The black paper absorbs heat, allowing you to cook your food from the bottom as well.

TAKE IT FURTHER

Add a thermometer inside your oven to measure exactly how hot your oven can get. At what temperature do your s'mores begin to cook? You can experiment with black fabric instead of black paper, or Mylar instead of foil. See which materials better harness the sun's energy and cook your food. You can also cook hot dogs or heat a plate of leftovers in your solar oven.

BUILD A PINHOLE SOLAR ECLIPSE VIEWER

We're not supposed to look directly at the sun, because the sun's rays can do serious damage to our eyes. Sometimes, this rule can be hard to follow—like during a solar eclipse, when something really cool is happening with the sun and we want to see it with our own eyes!

You can't look directly at the sun during an eclipse, but you can watch the eclipse right in your own backyard with a big box, foil, and some tape. You can also get a feel for the science of optics while you're at it.

MATERIALS NEEDED

Long cardboard box (a florist box works well)

Box cutter

Aluminum foil (cut to a 2.5" x 2.5" square)

Box cutter

Invisible tape

Thumbtack

White paper (cut to a 3" x 3" square)

Wide tape (masking tape, duct tape, or painter's tape)

PROCEDURE

1. On one of the ends of your cardboard box, cut a 2" x 2" square on the lower right corner.

2. On the outside of the box, cover your cut-out square with the square of aluminum foil. Use your invisible tape to secure your foil. Try to avoid wrinkling the foil.

3. Use your thumbtack to poke one small hole into the center of your aluminum foil square. The hole should be no wider than the point of your thumbtack.

4. On the inside of the other end of the box, tape your white paper square across from the aluminum square so that whatever light comes in through the pinhole will shine onto the white paper. This will serve as your "projection screen" where you will view the eclipse.

5. On the side of the box, just around the corner from the white paper square, you will want to cut a 3" x 3" square. This will allow you to view the projection screen at an angle without hurting your eyes.

6. Tape your box shut. Try to tape over any cracks or openings aside from your viewing square. You will want the only light entering your box to be from the pinhole you have created on your aluminum square.

7. Now it's time to use your solar viewer! You can test your viewer by standing outside and holding the box up so that it aligns with its own shadow. The pinhole should be pointing behind you toward the sun, and the viewing window should be out in front of you.

    If you have trouble seeing the sun on your piece of paper from this angle, you can adjust the viewing window by widening it with your box cutter.

When you have the opportunity to view a solar eclipse, stand with the box aligning with its own shadow. When you see the bead of light as it crosses your paper, that's the sun! Soon, you will see a shadow moving over the sun, this is the moon forming the eclipse as it passes between the sun and the Earth.

WHAT'S HAPPENING?

The small pinhole on the foil allows for the sunlight to be focused through a single point. The light waves expand as they travel through the box, which allows the image of the sun to be cast onto your viewing paper. The bigger the box, the larger the image that will be viewed through the window.

TAKE IT FURTHER

You can replicate this viewer with a smaller box, or you can find the largest box in your house to see which box will yield a larger image on your viewing window. Sometimes a city will host an eclipse viewing party with their local astronomical society. Take your solar eclipse viewer with you to enjoy the eclipse, and enjoy sharing the joy of astronomy with fellow amateurs and scientists in your community!

BUILDING a Spectrometer

When you step outside in the morning, the first thing you might notice is the bright light of the sun. The sun emits all the light we see and all of the energy we need to live on Earth. Scientists figured out that the sun is made up of primarily hydrogen and helium, but how did they figure that out? The answer has to do with rainbows! Every source of light emits its own color pattern based on the gases inside it. The study of this pattern is called spectrography.

You can make your own spectrometer and explore the light in your own home!

MATERIALS NEEDED

Cereal box

Ruler

Pen or pencil

Box cutter

Duct tape

Blank CD

Garden or kitchen shears

Flashlight, light bulb, and any other light sources around your house

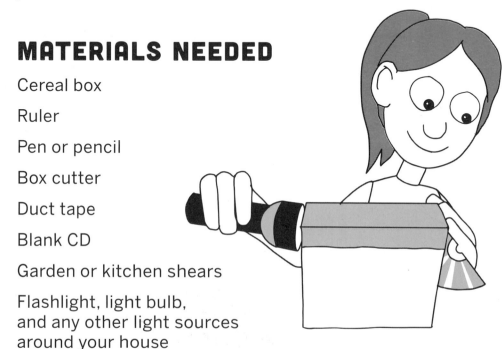

PROCEDURE

1. You're going to open a long rectangular section from the top right corner of your cereal box. Starting from the top corner of one side of your cereal box, use your ruler and pencil to mark a line 3 1/2" down from the top. Mark the same measurement on the other side of the box. Then measure 1" into the center of the box on both sides.

2. Use your box cutter to cut a rectangular section from the top of the box down to those markings (removing the side piece between your markings as you cut). This will make a little ledge on your cereal box for the CD to sit on.

3. On the other narrow side of the box, use your box cutter to cut a small horizontal slit approximately 1" down from the top. You'll want the slit to be fairly thin, only about 1 mm high. Cut the slit so that it spans the width of the side of the box.

4. Use your duct tape to seal the top of the cereal box that remains.

5. Put on your safety glasses because it's time to cut your CD in half! Use the garden shears to cut your CD in half. Use your scissors to trim away any excess pieces.

6. With the cut side of the CD facing away from the cereal box, place the CD on your ledge, glossy side facing up.

7. Shine your flashlight through the slit on the other side of the CD box. While holding your flashlight in place, tilt your CD up and down, until you find the angle in which your spectrum will show on your CD.

8. Once you have your spectrum showing on your CD, duct tape your CD in place.

9. Make sure you close in the sides of the ledge with the tape. This will allow less light to enter your spectrometer from the sides, and provide a sort of shadow box, with which you can view your spectra.

10. Test your light sources! Begin by examining the spectrum that can be emitted from your flashlight. Then, go outside and observe the spectrum from the sun! Tilt your spectrometer so that the small slit lines up with your light source. Then you can peer down onto your CD to see the color spectrum from that source.

WHAT'S HAPPENING?

It takes a lot of energy, and a lot of elements crashing together at high pressures and heat, for light to form. We can see this energy in the form of light waves. Our brain turns the light waves into colors that we can see. The light waves can look different, depending on gases that light passes through on its way to our eyes. The gases can absorb different wavelengths, leaving a black band through some of the colors. This is why you might see black spaces in your color spectrum on your spectrometer. In other cases, light is emitted from the burning of gases. These spectrum bands will have more solid color blocks, without any black lines. Take your spectrometer outside, to a friend's house, or anywhere you might find a variety of light sources. Bring the rainbow of the universe wherever you are!

TAKE IT FURTHER

There are many different light sources you can experiment with! You can use incandescent light bulbs, CFLs, the light from your computer and television screens, a UV flashlight, nightlight, or anything else you can find! When you look at light from different sources, you can really start to get a good idea of the different spectra that can be emitted from each light source.

DIG
PLANT
PLUCK

CHAPTER 2

SCIENCE IN THE GARDEN

Autumn Leaf
MASH-UP

When we hear the words fall or autumn, most people think of brilliantly colored leaves gently falling to the ground. But these colors can actually be found deep within the leaves all year long. During spring and summer, trees are busy producing chlorophyll, the molecule primarily responsible for photosynthesis (how a plant makes food). With this experiment, you'll discover the hidden colors within the leaves. All it takes is a few household materials and a little bit of chemistry.

MATERIALS NEEDED

An assortment of leaves

Scissors

3 glass jars

Paper and pen

Tape

91% isopropyl alcohol

Knife

Plastic wrap

Hot water

Shallow baking pan

White coffee filters

Bowl

Spoon

PROCEDURE

1. Go on a nature walk! Collect leaves from a variety of trees and get as many colors as you can. Try to identify the trees from which you're gathering them.

2. Choose three leaves you like and draw pictures of them to use as labels for your jars. Cut them out and tape them to the jars.

3. Using your scissors, cut and tear your leaves into very small pieces. Place one type of leaf into each of the three jars.

4. Cover the leaves with isopropyl alcohol. Then use your knife to stir and chop them into the solution. You want to break up the leaves as roughly as possible, so that the pigments can be drawn out by the alcohol.

5. Loosely cover your jars with plastic wrap, and place them into a shallow baking pan. Slowly pour about 1" of hot water into the bottom of your pan.

6. Keep the jars in the water for 30 minutes. Every 5-10 minutes, use your knife to roughly swirl the leaves around in the alcohol.

    Note: The hot water is what gets the molecules in the leaves moving faster through the alcohol. If you notice your water has grown cold, replace it with fresh hot water so you can keep those molecules moving!

7. Cut your coffee filters into long strips, about ½" wide. After 30 minutes, the alcohol will have changed color. Remove the plastic wrap and add your filters. Put one end of the strip into the alcohol solution and tape the other end of the strip to the top of the jar.

8. Leave your jars alone and let chromatography do its job! Wait approximately 90 minutes. During this time, the alcohol will start travelling up the coffee filter, carrying the molecules of the leaves with it. As it evaporates, the colors will stay on the filter. You'll end up with rainbows of yellows, reds, oranges, golds, browns, and greens, depending on the leaves you use!

WHAT'S HAPPENING?

Chlorophyll contains so much green pigment that all we can see is green in leaves. However, there are molecules within leaves that contain red and orange pigments. It's only when the seasons change that we see these colors, because trees stop producing chlorophyll during the colder months. Chromatography is a process that separates pigments and colors along a filter using alcohol. When they move up the paper, we can see the separate colors.

TAKE IT FURTHER

Can you find the same pigments in your leaves through the changing seasons of the year? Create a science journal to record your observations year round. Draw the shapes of the leaves you use, and color them with the colors you see. Conduct this experiment in winter, spring, summer, and fall, and record any changes in the pigments you observe.

May the Best Soil WIN

What makes a beautiful garden grow? We know that plants need sunlight, water, and soil, but what different soils are better for different plants? Some plants thrive in hard-packed soils, while others need plenty of drainage to grow and thrive. One thing all plants have in common is that they all need nutrients to grow. In this experiment, you'll determine the best soils and growing conditions for a bountiful garden.

MATERIALS NEEDED

4 small plastic cups

Scissors

Permanent marker

Paper

Tape

Clay soil

Potting mix

Sand

Pebbles

Radish seeds
(or other easy-to-grow seeds)

Pencil

Water

Ruler

PROCEDURE

1. Using your scissors, carefully poke 4 holes in the bottom of each plastic cup.

2. Using your permanent marker and paper, make labels for your cups. You should have a label for clay soil, potting mix, sand, and mixed soil (which you will make in the next step). Cut the labels out and tape them to the plastic cups. Fill each flower cup with its corresponding soil.

3. For your mixed soil, add a small amount of sand, clay, potting mix, and pebbles to the cup, and stir to thoroughly combine. Following the planting directions on the package of radish seeds, plant 4 seeds in each of the four cups.

4. Carefully water the cups, and then set your cups in an area that receives plenty of sunlight.

5. On a piece of paper, create a table so you can document any changes in your plants, and monitor their growth. Label the x axis of your table with the type of soils you're using, and the y axis with seven days of the week.

6. Each day, monitor the growth of your plants and document the changes you see on your table. As your plants begin to sprout, use your ruler to measure their growth.

7. Over the duration of a week, follow the germination rate of your plants, and observe which plants have grown the best in your soils. Then you can determine which type of soil is the best for your seeds!

WHAT'S HAPPENING?

The best kinds of soils contain a mix of rocks, sand, plant and animal matter, fungi, and manure. Soil that is full of these things will help a big, beautiful garden grow. If the dirt is unable to drain water well, the plants can drown in the dirt. If the dirt is unable to hold any water, the plant can't extract nutrients from the soil. Finding a balance is key!

Make Your Own Compost

What is soil made of? Many people might say rocks, or sand, or even dust. But the truth is: The richest soils are made of a lot of decomposed matter, including leaves, insects, decaying plant matter, bacteria, fruit scraps, and seeds. Plants take nutrients from the soil and then return those nutrients to the ground when they die. By creating a small amount of compost in your kitchen, you can see how the process of soil creation works. All you need is a bit of waste material, a little bit of chemistry, and a lot of time. You'll also be giving back to the Earth as you find an ecofriendly way to reuse your waste.

MATERIALS NEEDED

Organic matter
(leaves, fruit and vegetable scraps, grass clippings, egg shells, coffee grinds, etc.)

Large plastic cup

Scissors

Large bowl

Large spoon

2 tablespoons water

¼ cup soil

Plastic wrap

Rubber band

Small saucer

PROCEDURE

Collect a variety of compostable materials. These can include things like stems, flowers, fruit and vegetable peels, grass clippings, egg shells, coffee grinds, a whole host of things! Anything that grows from the ground can be used for compost.

NOTE: Stay away from meat and dairy products, as these will create an awful smell and may attract unwanted visitors to your compost.

8. Take your large cup and poke several holes in the bottom. Water will accumulate in your composting cup throughout the compost process and it will need a place to drain.

9. Using your scissors, cut the leaves and stems into small pieces and add them to the bowl. Combine the remaining compostable materials into the bowl and use your spoon to stir it all together.

10. Add 2 tablespoons of water to the compostable material, and then add ¼ cup of soil. Stir to thoroughly combine.

11. Use your spoon to scoop two heaping spoonfuls of compostable material into the large cup.

12. Cover the top of your compost cup with plastic wrap and use the rubber band to tightly seal it around the edges.

13. Find a nice warm spot to place your cup, where it will get lots of sun. Shake your cup around and set it in its new resting place with a small saucer beneath it to catch the draining water. Every few days, you'll need to add a tablespoon of water to your compost mix and shake it up a bit. This will make the bacteria work harder to decompose your plant matter and keep things moving!

WHAT'S HAPPENING?

Everywhere around us, you can find materials that are decaying and decomposing. As they break down, they become compost. Compost contains a ton of bacteria and chemical compounds, such as carbon, nitrogen, phosphorus, and potassium, that help plants grow and thrive. Composting is good for the environment because it feeds decomposed plants right back to the Earth.

Make a Leaf SKELETON

How do plants transport water and nutrients from their stems to their leaves? Plants have a network of veins and vessels that carry food, water, and minerals to various parts of their bodies. The network of veins is hidden within the plant. With this experiment, you can remove the layers of the leaf to find a skeleton of veins underneath.

This experiment requires the patience of a scientist. You will need to be careful in order to reveal the beautiful and delicate skeletons!

MATERIALS NEEDED

Waxy leaves

Latex or nitrile gloves

Laundry washing soda

Water

Metal pot

Large glass bowl

Tweezers

Bleach

Paper towels

Toothbrush

PROCEDURE

1. Go on a nature walk! Collect a variety of leaves, focusing on leaves that have a thick, waxy texture. Collect a few leaves that do not have a waxy texture so you can compare your results during this experiment.

2. Combine 2 cups of water and ½ cup of washing soda in a metal pot and bring to a boil.

    SAFETY NOTE: It is important to use a metal pot so the caustic washing soda doesn't cause an adverse chemical reaction.

3. Add your leaves and turn the heat down to a simmer. After approximately 20 minutes, add two more cups of water, then continue to simmer for about 90 minutes. Add water as needed, if it evaporates.

4. After approximately 2 hours of simmering, the water should look brown, with material floating on the surface. Remove the pot from heat, and fill a large bowl with cold water.

5. Gently remove the leaves with tweezers, and transfer them to the bowl filled with cold water. Let them sit in the water for 30 minutes. Then use your tweezers to gently remove them and place them on a paper towel.

6. Use your toothbrush to gently pat at the leaves, firmly pressing down all over the surface of the leaves. Use the brush in a gentle sweeping motion to remove the excess skin and pulp.

7. Turn the leaf over and repeat the process for the other side. Use your tweezers to remove any loose skin from the leaf that may be attached to the stem.

8. Continue to brush away the excess material until you begin to see the network of leaf veins emerge. Take care with the brush, as these veins are delicate and will break away if handled too roughly.

9. When the leaves have been fully skeletonized, have a parent put on gloves and transfer them to a bowl filled with bleach and submerge them for 20 minutes.

10. Have a parent remove the leaves (still wearing gloves) and set them on some paper towels to dry. Now you can admire the beautiful network of veins within the leaves that transport water and nutrients to various parts of the plant!

   SAFETY NOTE: Washing soda has a pH of 11, making it a very caustic substance that can irritate your hands if handled without protection. Make sure you wear your gloves in this experiment, and have an adult work with the washing soda.

WHAT'S HAPPENING?

Leaves are covered with a protective layer of skin called the epidermis. Washing soda is a substance that is used to remove laundry stains and mineral deposits. Because it has a high pH, it is very effective at dissolving substances. The highly caustic washing soda breaks down the epidermis in the leaves, exposing the tougher veins beneath.

TAKE IT FURTHER

Try this experiment with tough waxy leaves, as well as softer non-waxy leaves. Will the washing soda remove the skin in the same way, while still preserving the network of veins underneath? You can also try this with baking soda! Try the two materials and compare your results.

When finished, you can spray paint your leaf skeletons and use them for decorations, art projects, or gifts, or frame them to put on display!

Color-Changing Carnations

Plants need three things to survive: water, sunlight, and oxygen. How do plants get water from their roots to where it's needed? They seem to defy gravity to draw water up to their roots, stems, leaves, and flowers. Would they still be able to get water without roots? With this experiment, you'll explore how plants absorb water and nutrients, and direct it to where it's needed throughout the plant. You may even get a burst of colorful surprise, as you see where the water ends up!

MATERIALS NEEDED

3 tall glasses or small vases

Water

Red and green
(or two other different colors)
food coloring

Scissors

2 carnations

Knife

28

PROCEDURE

1. Fill one tall glass ¼ of the way with water, then add 10-20 drops of red food coloring, stirring to thoroughly combine.

2. Using your scissors, cut the stem of two of the carnations at a 45-degree angle, then place one flower in the water.

3. Leave your carnation and plan to observe it again in 24 hours. What will you see in the petals of the flowers? What will you see in the stem?

4. Using your knife, take the second carnation and split the stem lengthwise, right down the middle, approximately 4" from the bottom of the stem.

5. Fill two tall glasses with water. In one of the glasses, stir in 10 drops of green food coloring. In the other glass, stir in 10 drops of red food coloring.

6. Place one half of the stem in the red glass, and the other half of the stem in the green glass. You may need to place something behind the flower to prop it up while you wait and record your observations.

7. Observe the flower over a 48-hour period, and see if you can split your flower into two colors!

WHAT'S HAPPENING?

How do plants get water to travel all the way from their roots to the rest of the plant? The answer is capillary action. Water molecules are attracted to each other and cling together tightly. They don't bond with air, which causes them to form a bond of surface tension.

As the water molecules stick to the inside of the stem, the molecules next to them move up so they can maintain surface tension. The food coloring is mostly made of water, which sticks to the other water molecules and moves all the way up to the petals of your flower!

Build a
WATER FILTER
with Sand and Rocks

Water is essential for all life on Earth! With everything from drinking water to showers, agriculture, and everyday business use, we consume a lot of this precious resource. Where does it come from, and how do we get it to the faucets in our homes? How is this water safe to drink? You may be surprised to find that the Earth has a natural filtration process that people have learned to imitate when filtering water to make it safe to drink. In this experiment, you'll learn how to filter dirty water with, believe it or not, sand and rocks!

MATERIALS NEEDED

2-liter bottle with its cap

½ cup dirt

2 large (about 20-32 oz) cups

2-liter bottle, cut in half

2 tablespoons alum powder

Coffee filter

Rubber band

1 cup fine-grain play sand

½ cup activated charcoal
(found at most pet stores)

⅔ cup of coarse multi-use sand

1 cup of small, washed aquarium pebbles

1½ cups of large washed gravel

Large wide-mouthed glass
(that a 2-liter bottle can fit into)

Large spoon for stirring

1 liter of swamp water

PROCEDURE

1. To make your swamp water, fill your first 2-liter bottle halfway with water, and add ½ cup of dirt. Put the cap on the bottle and swirl the bottle around to mix the dirt into the water. Let it sit for a couple of hours so the dirt can thoroughly dissolve into the water.

2. After the water has turned a muddy brown, shake the bottle vigorously for about 30 seconds. This will help get some of the trapped gases out.

3. Pour the water into one of the large cups, and then pour it into the other cup. Continue pouring the water back and forth into each cup, about ten times. This will continue aerating the water during the water treatment process. Pay attention to how the water looks and smells. Do you think this water would be safe to drink?

4. Pour the water into the bottom half of your cut 2-liter bottle. Add 2 tablespoons of alum to the water and stir slowly for about 5 minutes. Observe the water as you stir, and make note of any changes to the water.

5. After 5 minutes, let the water sit undisturbed for approximately 20 minutes. Periodically check the water and make note of any changes that you see in the consistency of the water.

6. Begin making your filter by placing the coffee filter over the mouth of the top half of your cut 2-liter bottle. Use your rubber band to tightly secure the filter in place.

7. Pour the fine sand over the filtered plug in the bottle. Then add the activated charcoal, pouring it into an even layer over the sand. Slowly pour the coarse sand over the charcoal, making sure to keep the layers even. Then add the small pebbles, and fill the rest of the bottle with coarse gravel.

8. Set the filter into the wide glass vase, with the filter side down. Pour 2 cups of tap water into your filter to clean it out. Let it run until all the water has dripped through your filter and into your glass.

9. After all the water has dripped out of the filter, carefully lift it up, being careful not to disturb the layers, and dump out the water in the cup. Set the filter back in, and pour the swamp water through the filter. Observe and record the results.

WHAT'S HAPPENING?

You are making a water treatment plant! Your filter works the way water treatment plants filter water. During the filtration, the water travels through layers of rocks and sand, which remove particles from the water. The activated charcoal binds some of the particles, which form a film as the water passes through the charcoal.

SAFETY NOTE: This water is NOT safe to drink. While it is clear, it has not been sterilized. Sterilization is when bacteria and parasites are removed.

TAKE IT FURTHER

What kind of pollutants can your water treatment filter remove from your water? Try adding vegetable oil, food coloring, small bits of styrofoam, and other objects to your water. Then run this polluted water through your filter, and see what the filter is able to remove from the water. You can visit your local city's water treatment facilities to see how they filter and treat the water that you drink in your home.

STOMP

CHAPTER 3

PECK

AMAZING BUGS AND ANIMALS

SOAR

FOSSIL FOOTPRINTS

Every time you step outside, you are surrounded by life! From birds to lizards to rabbits, there is a wild world out there that scientists are always learning more about. Sometimes animals leave behind tracks, feathers, or bones that stay in the ground for days, weeks, or millions of years! When larger prehistoric animals roamed, they left footprints that sank deep into the soil. These tracks became fossilized and taught scientists a lot about animals that no longer exist. You can create your own "fossil" today, right in your kitchen.

MATERIALS NEEDED

Modeling clay

Hard plastic animal toys

Disposable bowl

Plaster of Paris

Cold water

Wooden paint stick or plastic knife

Large plastic cup

PROCEDURE

1. Work the modeling clay with your hands until it becomes soft and pliable. Press it into a flat circle that is approximately ½" thick.

2. Take an assortment of animal toys, and firmly press their feet down into the clay, creating deeply set footprints. Make sure the footprints are evenly spaced apart in your clay.

3. Place the clay into the bottom of your disposable bowl, gently pressing on the edges so it creates a tight seal.

4. To mix the plaster of Paris, pour ½ cup of cold water into the large plastic cup. Then pour 1 cup of plaster into the water. Use your plastic knife or wooden stirring stick to thoroughly mix the plaster.

   SAFETY NOTE: Be careful not to breathe in any of the plaster particles! They bond with water over time, and would not be pleasant to have inside your lungs.

5. Once the plaster is thoroughly mixed, slowly pour the mixture over your clay. Pour an even layer, making sure that there is at least ½" between the plaster and the top of the bowl.

6. Wait approximately 30 minutes for the plaster to begin to set. Then move it into a cool, dry place where it can continue to set overnight.

7. After 24 hours, peel the bowl away from the sides of your plaster, then gently peel the clay away from the plaster. Admire your creation, as you now own a set of fossils that you have created!

WHAT'S HAPPENING?

When prehistoric animals like dinosaurs roamed the Earth, they left footprints in the ground. Over time, these footprints were filled with small pebbles, sand, and other sediments, as layers of earth built on top of each other over millions of years. Sometimes the layers are brought to the surface by upheaval, when the ground shifts upwards. When this happens, footprints, imprints, and even fossilized bones can be brought to the surface.

Darwin's FINCHES

When Charles Darwin studied animals on the islands of Galapagos, he learned a lot about how animals have adapted (or changed) to handle their environments. This understanding began with the beaks of several birds called finches. The finches' beaks were different, depending on where they lived and what they ate. With this experiment, you too can observe the differences in the beaks of birds, and discover which beaks are best suited for various types of foods. All you need are some kitchen utensils and a variety of foods.

MATERIALS NEEDED

BEAKS:

Toothpick (Woodpecker)

Straw (Hummingbird)

Pliers (Finch)

Tweezers (Mourning Dove)

Slotted spoon (Duck)

Skewer (Heron)

FOOD:

Rubber bands (Worms)

Cheese cut into small cubes (Insects)

Lunch meat (Fish)

Seeds, beans, pretzels (Seeds)

Rice, noodles, oats in water (Water insects, algae)

Juice (Nectar)

MISCELLANEOUS:

Shallow bowls and cups

Paper

Pencil

PROCEDURE

1. Line up your beaks on one side of your table. On the other side, set up a variety of bowls and cups.

2. Set up your plates and bowls. Place the various items in a separate bowl or cup. Line up the "beaks" next to the food.

3. Take a look at the different "beaks" that are on the table. Which beaks would be the best for each type of food?

4. Pick up a beak and match it to the appropriate bird. Then find the food you think it could easily pick up with its beak. Write down your guesses. When you think you have them all matched up correctly, check them against the answers in the paragraph below.

WHAT'S HAPPENING?

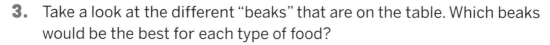

Many birds have different types of beaks that suit their needs, depending on what they eat and where they get it. Finches have cone-shaped bills that help them crack seeds like a pair of pliers. Mourning doves and other insect eaters have thin, pointed beaks that work like tweezers to grab hidden insects. Hummingbird beaks are long like a straw to help them suck the nectar from flowers. Herons and other spear fishers use their long spear-shaped beaks to catch fish. For woodpeckers, their beaks work like chisels to poke into wood like a toothpick and help them suck out bugs with their tongue. Finally, ducks have strainer beaks that work like slotted spoons to help them sift through water for their food.

The Ants Go MARCHING

Most people communicate with each other by voice, or by body language, but did you know there is a way to communicate using a scent trail? Animals have a chemical language built into their bodies. These chemicals are called pheromones, and animals release these chemical messages to communicate all sorts of things. In this experiment, you can see a scent trail in action and even try making one of your own!

MATERIALS NEEDED

Partner

Sponge

A strongly scented oil, perfume, or air freshener spray

Tile floor, or make a big paper trail out of construction paper

Blindfold

Piece of paper

Ants

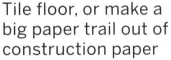

PROCEDURE

1. Go outside and soak your sponge with a strong-smelling substance. Doing this outside will prevent the odor from overwhelming the room in which you will conduct your experiment.

2. While your partner is in another room, wipe the sponge along the floor, making a trail of scent. Be sure to thoroughly soak your surface so that the scent will create a path along your surface.

3. Bring your partner in the room and secure the blindfold around his eyes.

4. Have your partner get on his hands and knees near the beginning of your trail. Watch as he seeks out the pheromone trail and follows exactly where you've placed it. You can even join in the fun, too, as you demonstrate how ants follow the chemical messages of scouts to find their food.

5. Trade places! Have your partner follow these instructions and lay out another trail in a separate area. How well will you be able to find the chemical messages?

6. Now take a piece of paper and head outside to look for an ant trail. Once you've found a trail of ants moving to and from their home, brush aside a section of their trail and set your paper down in front of them.

7. The ants will soon begin to make a new trail of pheromones over your paper. Once they have formed another trail with ants marching in a straight line over the paper, rotate the paper by 90 degrees. Will the ants march in the same direction? Or will they continue to follow their phero-mone path to a new destination?

WHAT'S HAPPENING?

In an ant colony, ants lay a chemical trail (called pheromones) as they hunt for food, allowing other ants to find the food once it's discovered. As other ants traverse the trail, they lay their own pheromones down on top of the scouts', strengthening the scent even further. Most animals are able to pick up these chemical messages in their noses, but ants sense them with their antennae.

Bright Lights AND Buggy Nights

Do you ever sit outside at night, under the lights in your yard? You may notice that you are soon surrounded by moths and that other insects start buzzing around you. Why are insects attracted to lights? With this experiment, you'll learn about the navigation of insects, how scientists and entomologists lure them to identify and study them, and how to use light to your advantage to create your own insect lure! With bright lights and buggy nights, you'll be well on your way to the study of entomology as you discover the fascinating world of invertebrates all around you!

MATERIALS NEEDED

Large white bed sheet

Rope

4 clothespins

Big flashlight

Optional: UV flashlight

Thick yarn

Magnifying glass

Paper and pencil

PROCEDURE

1. Find a nice wide spot in a backyard or neighborhood park, away from house lights or heavy foot traffic. Look for a wall, a chain fence, or fence posts that you can use to hang your sheet. If you can't find a fence, look for two trees that are close together so that you can use the piece of rope to secure your sheet.

2. Hang your sheet up over the rope, and use the clothespins to attach it securely. You can also use the clothespins to attach the sheet to a fence or wooden posts.

3. Use the yarn to hang your flashlight from the top of the fence or the rope itself, so that it hangs near the top of your sheet.

4. Turn on your flashlight and step back. Before long, you will begin to see moths, lacewings, beetles, and other nocturnal invertebrates fly to-wardsthe light and land on your sheet.

5. Use your magnifying glass to get a closer look at your nocturnal visitors and use your pen and paper to draw what you see!

6. Many insects see light from the ultraviolet spectrum. If you have an ultraviolet flashlight, try it with your sheet. If you collect insects with a regular flashlight one night and a UV light the next, will you notice a difference in the number and type of insects you attract?

WHAT'S HAPPENING?

Insects are attracted to bright lights! Nocturnal insects have a built-in navigation system that is based upon the light of the moon. They use that light to angle themselves on a path as they fly about, searching for food. Our modern artificial lights throw off their sense of direction. They fly close to the light to help them figure out where it's coming from and then lose their way because the light is coming from all sides.

Finding Life in a Drop of Water

If you were to look outside for wildlife, would you ever think to look in a puddle on the ground? Water is full of life! In a puddle, you can find swimming larvae, bacteria, and even plant life. You may not be able to see all this life within a single drop of water, but if you put it under the microscope, suddenly the world of microbial life comes into focus! All you need is a dropper, a collection vial, and a microscope, and you will be on your way to discovering a tiny, amazing universe of living creatures!

MATERIALS NEEDED

Medicine droppers

Microscope

Microscope slide and slip cover

Test tube

Permanent marker

Pencil

Paper

PROCEDURE

1. Take a medicine dropper and collect a sample of water from a puddle. Drip the sample into your test tube and label it with where you found it.

2. When you get home, take your medicine dropper and put one drop from your puddle onto a microscope slide. Cover it with your slipcover.

3. Look at your slide through the microscope. Immediately, you'll be immersed in the tiny universe of microscopic organisms. While they're too small to see with the naked eye, with some precise magnification their busy world is brought to life right before your eyes.

4. Draw what you see through the lens of your microscope. You might see blocky chains of algae, the green and red of algae and bacterium, or circular swimming diatoms. You might even find twisting insect larvae, or maybe even a paramecium! See what is going on in this busy world in front of you.

WHAT'S HAPPENING?

Millions of microorganisms are out there just waiting to be discovered. Some microbes can be harmful to humans (so don't swallow this water), but others can provide a huge benefit. Due to the predator/prey relationship of some microorganisms, they can make our water drinkable. Microbes are a fundamental part of life on Earth.

TAKE IT FURTHER

You can collect samples from different locations and compare the life you find. Make sure you use separate droppers and test tubes for each location. What similarities and differences can you find in the environments? Document your journey with a science journal! Draw the organisms you see, and make a note of the date and location for each.

Build an INSECT HOTEL

With this activity, you will head outside, get dirty, and build a home for the amazing insects in your backyard or garden. Take delight in the antics of a jumping spider chasing its prey. Marvel at the colors of a beetle's wing in the sunlight. Entice ladybugs and lacewings and watch as the beautiful world of insects thrives right under your fingertips. Grab your magnifying glass, some gardening gloves, and some leaf clutter, and build an insect hotel for these interesting critters!

MATERIALS NEEDED

8 12" lengths of scrap wood boards

Pine needles

Pine cones

Sticks and bark

Leaves

2 bricks

Small flower pot

Shovel

Scissors

Cardboard

Long seeds

Flowers, weeds, discarded plants

Construction paper

Fruit peels and vegetable scraps

PROCEDURE

1. Gather scrap wood, either from scrapped pallets, scrap lumber from a hardware store, or from repurposed wooden boxes, cabinets, or a large birdhouse.

2. Go on a nature walk to collect organic material from your neighborhood! Take a basket and gather large sticks, handfuls of pine needles, 2 handfuls of pine cones, seeds, leaves, and anything else you can find lying on the ground.

3. Find a good spot in your garden (but not too close to your house, since you'll be attracting wood-boring beetles) to begin constructing your insect hotel. This can be located near bushes, flowering plants, or near an herb garden. Wherever you build your insect hotel, you can expect to find a lot of beneficial insects living nearby, and you'll want them to populate your garden.

4. Lay two bricks down flat on the ground, about 12" apart, and lay a thick layer of pine needles in between them to form a solid bedding.

5. Over the pine needles, lay two boards flat across the needles, so that they reach the bricks. Then, stand three thick boards on their sides, laying them lengthwise across the two flat boards, to that they make two columns in the middle.

6. Fill one of the columns halfway with seeds, and the other half with flowers and plant material. Do the same with the other side, making sure that the materials fill up the columns up to the top of the boards.

7. Cut wide strips of cardboard so they will fit across the top of your seed layer. Lay them over your seeds and plant material, making sure they reach across to cover the boards.

8. Lay three thick boards on their sides, forming two columns on top of the cardboard. Make rolled paper tubes with your construction paper, rolling lengthwise, and fill one column with the tubes. Fill the other column with large pieces of bark and sticks.

9. Now, cover your paper and bark columns with a waterproof roofing material. You can use cardboard, wood, or waxy leaves to make a roof for your hotel! Add a layer of pine cones on top.

10. To decorate around the edges of the hotel, you can fill flower pots with pine needles or extra bark and sticks to provide other crevices for little critters to make their homes in. Place fruit peels around the bottom of the hotel to entice decomposers to come and visit your hotel!

WHAT'S HAPPENING?

The many layers in your insect hotel attract beneficial visitors to your garden! The bark and sticks attract larvae of wood-boring beetles. As the wood is broken down by fungi, small holes can become homes for centipedes and wood lice. The leaf litter provides safe places for worms, ants, ladybugs, and more. The insects your hotel can attract also benefit your garden. Some of them prey on harmful parasites.

TAKE IT FURTHER

Grab a magnifying glass and a science journal, and make drawings of the insects you see in your hotel!

SPLISH

CHAPTER 4

SPLASH

COOL KITCHEN EXPERIMENTS

SWIRL

SQUISHING OUT STRAWBERRY DNA!

Every living thing on Earth is made up of cells: tiny, microscopic building blocks for life! It takes a lot of cells to make something like a person, a flower, or a tree. For a cell to know what it needs to build, it needs instructions. These instructions are called DNA (deoxyribonucleic acid). DNA is locked up deep inside the nucleus of every cell, protected by cell walls, membranes, and other strong barriers. It contains all the genetic instructions for every cell in your body! With common household ingredients, we can break it free and see it for ourselves!

MATERIALS NEEDED

3 large strawberries

Plastic sandwich bag

90 ml of water

15 ml of liquid dish soap

1 tsp salt

Strainer or cheesecloth

Small glass bowl

Spoon

10 ml cold 91% isopropyl alcohol

Cup

Wooden skewer

Safety goggles

PROCEDURE

TIP: The night before you do your lab, put your bottle of isopropyl alcohol in the freezer. The colder the alcohol gets, the better the DNA extraction works.

1. A good scientist always begins with proper lab safety! Put on your safety goggles before you begin your experiment. Then, place your strawberries in a plastic bag. Seal the bag closed, then break down the strawberries by pressing with your fingers until there are no longer any large pieces.

2. Combine the water, salt, and dish soap in a cup. Gently stir to thoroughly mix the ingredients. Then reopen the bag and add your solution to the bag. Close the bag, making it as airtight as possible.

3. Using your hands and fingers, mash and squish the strawberries and the solution together for approximately two minutes. When you are finished, you should see what looks like a slightly foamy strawberry soup.

4. Slowly pour the strawberry mixture through a strainer and into a small glass bowl. Use your spoon to press against the strawberries, getting as much liquid as possible through the strainer and into the bowl.

5. Slowly pour the cold isopropyl alcohol down the side of your bowl and into the strawberry mixture. You will begin to see a separation of layers as the alcohol rests on top of the water.

6. Observe this mixture for approximately two minutes. You should begin to see some white strands form over the top of your mixture. This is strawberry DNA!

7. Using the wooden skewer, slowly skim the surface of the liquid. As the white strands cling to the skewer, roll it up to draw out the DNA. This gooey substance is a mixture of DNA and the proteins that held it together within the cells!

WHAT'S HAPPENING?

Strawberries contain eight copies of each type of chromosome in their DNA. By contrast, human cells only contain two copies of each type of chromosome. The soap and water work together to break down the cell walls of the plant cells. The salt binds to the proteins that lock the DNA in place, allowing us to break those down, too. Finally, DNA is not soluble in alcohol, which means that it will not dissolve in it. When the alcohol is cold, it allows the DNA strands to quickly clump together and rise to the surface!

TAKE IT FURTHER

While the DNA will still be too small to see with the naked eye, you can still get a good look at the long strands under the microscope! You will not be able to see the helices; however, you will see the long strands of chained-up DNA molecules. In each cell, there are about 15 feet of DNA tightly wound together!

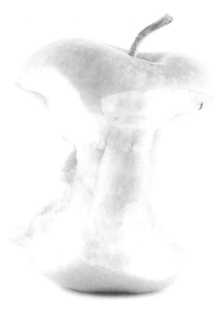

Rotten APPLE CHEMISTRY

Have you ever cut into a perfectly crisp apple, only to find that it starts to turn brown after just a couple of minutes? Why do our apples turn brown after they've been cut? Is there any way we can prevent that from happening so we can continue to enjoy these delicious fruits? With this experiment, you'll learn the chemistry behind browning apples, and you'll learn how you can use that chemistry to keep your apples fresh all day long. All you need are some kitchen acids, some household chemistry, and a healthy appetite!

MATERIALS NEEDED

3 index cards

Markers

3 apples

Vegetable peeler

Spoon

Butter knife

1 cup of lemon juice

Salt

Large bowl

Paper towel

Yarn

Paper clips

PROCEDURE

1. Using your markers, label your index cards with the materials you will be using in your experiment. On one card, write "lemon juice"; on another, "salt"; and finally, "control" on the last card.

2. Peel one of the apples, removing as much of the skin as you can. Then, use the butter knife and spoon to dig out the core from the bottom of the apple. Make sure to remove all seeds from inside the apple.

3. Mix the lemon juice and 2 tablespoons of salt in a glass bowl. Soak your apple in the bowl for three minutes, then flip it over and soak the other side for another three minutes. Pat it dry and set it aside. Place your "lemon juice" card in front of the apple.

4. Peel the second apple, making sure to remove as much of the skin as possible. Once again, use the knife and spoon to dig out the core and remove the seeds.

5. Thoroughly cover this apple with salt and rub the salt into the apple. Pour salt all over the surface, including the inside of the core. Once the salt is thoroughly covered, pat the apple to press the salt in, and then set it behind the "salt" card.

6. Finally, thoroughly peel and core the last apple, then set it behind of the "control" card. Since this is the control, this will be the apple you will compare your results to, so you won't be doing anything to this apple.

7. Drying methods: If the weather is warm and dry, use the yarn to hang the apples up outside for approximately one week.

Secure your index cards to the yarn with a paper clip so you can remember which method was used on each apple. Additional moisture may cause the apples to mold, so if rain is in your forecast, bring the apples inside! Alternatively, you can dry your apples inside by hanging them in a warm, dry area for approximately one week. Make sure it is hanging up high and out of reach of any critters who may be looking for a snack! Check your apples' progress every day. It will be finished when they are dry, spongy, hardened, and wrinkled.

8. Inspect your apples and compare them. Write down your observations. Which of the apples stayed the whitest? Could you use these results to help you pack apple slices for lunch?

WHAT'S HAPPENING?

When we cut into fruits and vegetables, we break the cells. Some fruits release enzymes from the broken cells. The enzymes react with each other and the air, turning the apple brown like it did with the control apple. In this experiment, the oxygen in the air reacted with the compounds in the lemon juice instead of the apple, slowing the browning process. The salt preserved your apple by drying it out, which deactivated the enzymes inside of it and also reduced browning. To preserve apples for snack time, just sprinkle some lemon juice over your apple slices or soak them in a salt water solution!

TAKE IT FURTHER

Try soaking your apples in a variety of liquids to see which ones will preserve your apple the best. You can also use this experiment to make shrunken apple heads! Use your knife to carve out a face in one apple before you soak it in lemon juice. Let it hang to dry for a week or two. Use this to make a homemade doll, or a fun decoration for Halloween!

DISAPPEARING EGGSHELLS

Have you ever wanted to know what an eggshell is made of, or to peek inside of an egg without cracking it open? With a little bit of chemistry, you can dissolve the eggshell and see what's underneath—and work as a scientist in your own kitchen. Grab an egg and some vinegar, and get ready to explore acids and bases as you dissolve your egg's mysterious shell.

MATERIALS NEEDED

Tall glass jar

Vinegar

One uncooked egg

Refrigerator

PROCEDURE

1. Fill a tall glass jar with vinegar. Make sure there is enough in there to completely submerge an egg.

2. Gently place your egg into the jar. You will immediately notice a change in the eggshell. Bubbles form from the vinegar interacting with the base in the calcium carbonate! In fact, the bubbles are pockets of carbon dioxide gas that have been separated from the calcium carbonate.

3. Observe your egg in the jar over the next 30 minutes. Note any differences on the surface of the egg, as well as the position of the egg. Is it still at the bottom of the jar, or has it begun to float near the surface?

4. Continue to check your egg throughout the day, making sure to notice any changes in the shell, or in the position of the egg in the jar. Place the jar in your refrigerator overnight.

5. The next morning, observe your egg again. Do you see any changes to the shell or position of the egg? After examining your egg, carefully pour the vinegar out into the sink. Add a fresh amount of vinegar to the jar, and place the jar back in your refrigerator for another 24 hours.

6. Finally, take your egg out of its jar. Carefully hold it in your hands. What does it feel like? What does it look like? You should see a significant change in your egg, especially if you compare it to another raw egg.

WHAT'S HAPPENING?

An egg is surrounded by a calcium eggshell. This calcium has a high pH, meaning it's a base. If we bring an acid in contact with the shell, the acid breaks down the calcium shell and the egg floats to the surface. When the shell has completely dissolved, it leaves a transparent membrane, allowing you to see the yolk inside. Why does your egg get larger? The egg grows in size because it absorbs the vinegar from the jar.

A DISH OF DANCING RAINBOWS

Did you know you can create a spectacular rainbow dance party in your kitchen, using a couple of kitchen ingredients? All you need is milk, food coloring, and dish soap, and you're on your way to dancing with rainbows! With this experiment, you can explore the science of surface tension, milk fats, and hydrophobic (water-repellent) substances.

MATERIALS NEEDED

Dinner plate

Whole or 2% milk

Food coloring

Dish soap

Cotton swab

PROCEDURE

1. Pour milk onto your dinner plate until it's completely covered.

2. Using a variety of colors, add drops of food coloring to the milk, spacing them evenly on the surface.

3. Soak the end of a cotton swab in dish soap, making sure the entire tip is evenly coated.

4. Gently touch the tip of the cotton swab to the surface of the milk. Observe what happens to the colors on the surface.

5. Move the cotton swab to various places on your dinner plate. Watch the colors dance and swirl as the colors, milk, and water interact with the detergent!

6. Once you are finished dabbing your cotton swab on your plate, wait for the colors to stop moving. Observe how they look on the plate. Do they look the same as when you started? Why do you think they look different?

WHAT'S HAPPENING?

Milk is made up of water, proteins, and fats. Because the milk is mostly water, it has surface tension, meaning the water molecules stick together. When we add emulsifying dish soap, it breaks the surface tension. The soap separates all the fats, proteins, and water molecules as you watch! Food coloring helps us to easily see this process in action.

TAKE IT FURTHER

Will this experiment work with all kinds of milk? Try it with skim or 1% milk. You can also test the effects of different temperatures. Try it with cold milk, then try it again with warm milk. Does this change the rate of swirling with your colors?

Cabbage-Water CHEMISTRY

Acids and bases are everywhere. Hydrochloric acid breaks down food in our stomach, and is so strong that it can dissolve certain metals. We can even find acids in our kitchen, in the form of vinegar, soda, and juices. We can also find bases in baking ingredients, household cleaners, and soaps! Scientists can tell the acidic or basic properties of a substance by using an indicator, which is something that changes color in the presence of an acid or a base. You can make an indicator at home, using some common household ingredients.

MATERIALS NEEDED

2 cups of finely chopped red cabbage

Hot water

Pyrex or other large heat-resistant bowl

Strainer

Pitcher

Vinegar

Baking powder

Ammonia-based household cleaner

3 cups

PROCEDURE

1. Take two cups of finely chopped cabbage and place them in the heat-resistant bowl. Cover with hot water and let stand for approximately 10 minutes. Observe as the water changes color as the pigments of cabbage seep into the water.

2. Pour the cabbage water through a strainer and into the pitcher. Discard the solid cabbage pieces.

3. Pour even amounts of cabbage water into three cups.

4. Now, it's time to test the ingredients! Pour a small amount of vinegar into the first cup. Pour a small amount of baking powder into the second cup and stir to mix thoroughly. Finally, pour the cleaner into the third cup.

5. You will notice the cabbage water changes color as you add the test ingredients. This demonstrates how the cabbage pigments can indicate the presence of an acid or a base.

WHAT'S HAPPENING?

Red cabbage contains pigments that change color in the presence of acids or bases, reflecting pink or red in the presence of an acid; or blue, green, or yellow in the presence of a base. You can match your colors to numbers on the pH scale. Strong acids and bases will be at the far ends of the spectrum, while weak acids and bases will be closer to the middle.

TAKE IT FURTHER

Can you make a rainbow of acids and bases in your kitchen? Try experimenting with a variety of materials, and see what colors of the pH scale you can create! You can use items like milk, lemon juice, soda, laundry detergent, and more, to test the acidity or alkalinity of substances around your home.

30

20

10

FABRIC ART
with Acids and Bases

Did you know you can create beautiful works of art with chemistry? In this experiment, you'll combine science and art with the exploration of acids and bases and create your very own watercolor painting that you can hang on your wall!

MATERIALS NEEDED

2 cups of finely chopped red cabbage

2 large bowls

Hot water

Strainer

100% cotton fabric

Pen

3 plastic cups

Vinegar

Baking powder mixed with water

Ammonia-based cleaner

Medicine dropper

SAFETY NOTE: Please make sure that the chemicals you are using will not cause a harmful reaction. Do NOT use bleach, as this can cause a harmful reaction when mixed with ammonia-based cleaners.

PROCEDURE

1. Finely chop two cups of red cabbage, and place them in a bowl. Pour hot water over the cabbage until it is completely submerged, and let soak for ten minutes.

2. Pour the cabbage in through a strainer, into the second bowl. Discard the solid pieces of cabbage, leaving only the liquid in the bowl.

3. Take the 100% cotton material and place it in the bowl, allowing it to soak in the colored liquid for 30 minutes.

4. Remove the fabric and hang it up outside to dry. Once your fabric is dried, you will have indicator fabric!

5. Once you're ready to create your masterpiece, draw a picture with your pen onto your fabric. Large shapes and designs are preferable, as you will be creating a watercolor masterpiece with your chemistry painting!

6. Pour the liquids into three separate cups. Vinegar will turn your fabric red, while baking powder will turn it blue, and the cleaner will turn it green.

7. Using the medicine dropper, place the liquids wherever you'd like on your painting. Watch as the colors blend and change the color of your fabric, based on the presence of acids and bases!

WHAT'S HAPPENING?

Red cabbage has a pigment that turns colors when it interacts with acids and bases. Acids will turn it red, while bases will turn it green or yellow. Water and other pH-neutral liquids will turn it blue. When you soak your cotton in the cabbage water, the pigment dyes the fabric. What you're left with is a fabric canvas that reacts to acids and bases with brilliant splashes of color.

Liquid Rainbow
TOWER

You can stack blocks, but did you know you can stack liquids too? Substances built with tightly packed molecules are denser than those built with molecules that are spread farther apart. Because of this, you can have different materials that are the same size and shape, but have different weights. All you need are some liquids and a tall glass jar, and you can build a liquid, rainbow tower in your kitchen!

MATERIALS NEEDED

Large glass jar

¼ cup of honey

¼ cup of light corn syrup

¼ cup of maple syrup

¼ cup of dish soap

¼ cup of water

¼ cup of vegetable oil

¼ cup of isopropyl alcohol

Food coloring

TIP: As you pour the liquids into your jar, make sure to pour very slowly and in the center of the jar. This layering takes patience and a steady hand, but the results are a dazzling liquid, rainbow tower!

PROCEDURE

1. Pour the honey into the bottom of your glass jar. Allow it to settle so it's evenly distributed along the bottom.

2. Slowly pour the corn syrup into the center of the honey. You will see layers begin to form as the less dense syrup comes to rest on top of the honey.

3. After the layers settle, slowly begin to pour the maple syrup directly in the center of the corn syrup.

4. Next, slowly pour the dish soap into the center of the maple syrup. You will see another layer start to form. Allow the dish soap to settle into place before moving on the to the next step.

5. Slightly tilt your jar to the side and very slowly pour the water down the side of the jar. Be very slow with this step, to avoid soap mixing and foaming with the water. When you finish pouring, set the jar back down on the table.

6. Take the vegetable oil and very slowly pour it into the center of the water. Make sure it pours in a very small stream, so that it doesn't push through the water and disturb the soap.

7. Finally, add some food coloring to the isopropyl alcohol. Then slowly pour that on top of the vegetable oil. If the liquids begin to mix a little, don't worry. They'll settle themselves into their layers, based on their density.

WHAT'S HAPPENING?

Density is a measure of how much "stuff" is in something. That "stuff" includes atoms and molecules that make up the mass of an object. The liquids that you add to your column all have different densities. That's why they separate into layers from most dense (bottom) to least dense (top).

SINKING AND FLOATING EGGS

Have you ever put an egg in a pot of water and watched it sink? Why doesn't it float? The answer has to do with density. Density is a measure of how tightly packed an object's molecules are. Everything in the universe is made up of atoms and molecules, and how closely they're all squished together determines the mass of an object. See if you can make that sinking egg float by experimenting with its density!

MATERIALS NEEDED

3 tall glass jars

Water

3 uncooked eggs

¼ cup salt

¼ cup sugar

Spoon

PROCEDURE

1. Fill all three jars ¾ of the way with water. Gently put an egg in one of the jars. This is your control. Since you aren't adding anything to it, this can be the normal egg to which you will compare your other eggs. Observe its position in the jar. Is it at the top or the bottom?

2. Add the salt to one of the remaining jars. Stir to dissolve and thoroughly mix into the water. Then gently place your second egg into the jar. Note its position as well, whether it is at the top or bottom of the jar.

3. Finally, add the sugar to the last jar. Stir to dissolve and thoroughly mix into the water. Gently place your egg into the jar. Note its position, whether it is at the top or bottom of the jar.

WHAT'S HAPPENING?

When you place your egg into the jar of water, it sinks to the bottom. That's because the water has a lower density than the egg! When you add the salt and sugar to the water, suddenly there is a lot more "stuff" in the water and that increases the water's density. When the water's density becomes greater than the egg's, the egg floats!

TAKE IT FURTHER

Will this experiment work with other liquids and materials as well? What if you added oil instead of water; would you still have the same result? Could you add something heavier, like a nail, and make that rise to the surface by increasing the density of the water? Give it a try!

NIBBLE

CHAPTER 5

CHEW

THE SCIENCE OF CANDY

CRUNCH

CANDY
Chromatography

Everything from a flower, to the sky, to the foods we eat, is an example of the color spectrum! Sometimes, the colors aren't quite what they seem, and this is especially true when looking at colors found in manmade items like candy. Looking at a candy-coated shell, you may see reds, blues, greens, oranges, or a variety of other colors. However, what makes the colors shine may surprise you! In this experiment, we're going to peel away the colors to find out what makes this tasty rainbow shine as we explore the science of chromatography.

MATERIALS NEEDED

Water

Small cup or wide-mouthed jar

¼ tsp of salt

White coffee filter

Pencil

Pen

Scissors

Aluminum foil

Pipette or medicine dropper

Skittles, one of each color

5 toothpicks

Tape

PROCEDURE

1. Pour ¼ cup of water into your cup. Add ¼ tsp of salt and stir to thoroughly combine.

2. Cut a coffee filter into a flat 3" x 3" square. On the bottom of the filter paper, ½" from the bottom, use the pencil to draw a line across the paper. Draw five small circles, evenly spaced apart, across the line on the filter paper.

3. Cut a strip of aluminum foil into a strip that is 8" long and 3" wide. Flatten out any wrinkles and use your pen to draw five circles, evenly spaced apart on the foil strip.

4. Using the pipette, place 2 drops of water on to each circle on the aluminum foil.

5. Place one color of Skittles candy onto each drop of water, and allow it to sit there for approximately one minute, while the colored dye dissolves into the water on the foil.

6. Remove the Skittles from the foil and discard them. Using one toothpick for each color, dab several drops of each color onto one of the small circles on your filter paper. Make sure you dab only one color on each circle.

7. Tape the top of your filter paper to your pencil. Lower the filter paper into the cup so that the water is just barely touching the bottom of the filter paper. Make sure that the water is below the line you drew on your filter paper.

8. Rest the pencil over the top of the glass. Allow the filter paper to rest in the water for approximately 30 minutes. Watch as capillary action draws the water up the filter paper, carrying the colors with it! Over time, you should see the separation of colors in your candies as the water crosses over the filter paper!

WHAT'S HAPPENING?

Chromatography is a way of separating a substance and identifying its components as it travels along a path and is absorbed at different rates. As the candy water crosses the filter paper, some of the color molecules are deposited on the paper. Different molecules are deposited at different rates, leaving different shades of color behind. Chromatography can help scientists and police detectives do all sorts of cool things, like analyze blood samples, identify bank robbers, and determine what pen was used to write a letter!

TAKE IT FURTHER

Try this experiment with different candies. Will the color reading of M&Ms be the same as what you see with Skittles? What about Nerds, or other colorful candies? Devise an experiment with different candy coatings to see how they all stand up to candy chromatography!

INSIDE A Gobstopper

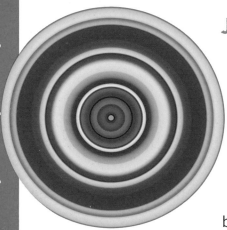

Jawbreakers have many layers of candy within their candy shells. What would happen if you were to drop a jawbreaker into a bowl of water? Would you be able to see the colors as they dissolved, or would they all blend into one big colorful mess? With this experiment, you'll explore the colorful world of candy and learn what helps a jawbreaker keep its layers.

MATERIALS NEEDED

Petri dish or shallow plate

Water

Gobstopper candy

Salt

PROCEDURE

1. Pour just enough water in your petri dish to cover the bottom evenly.

2. Separate your Gobstopper candies into separate colors. You'll want one of each color for the dish.

3. Place three to four Gobstoppers of different colors as far apart as possible in the dish. They should be no more than half submerged in the water, and they should be evenly spaced apart. They should not touch each other.

4. Observe your Gobstoppers as each colored layer dissolves into the water. What do you see happening with the layers? Are they evenly mixing into the water, or are they stopping?

5. Now try the experiment again, only this time, add salt to your water! Do you notice a difference in how the candies dissolve?

WHAT'S HAPPENING?

Candy has a layer of edible wax on the surface. This is what prevents it from melting in your hands. The wax doesn't dissolve into water. As the Gobstoppers dissolve, the wax forms a boundary between each color. When you add salt, it breaks down the wax. This is how you can witness each color dissolving. There's no longer a solid wax layer forming the boundary between each coating!

TAKE IT FURTHER

Does every colored candy dissolve in this way? Experiment with M&Ms, Skittles, and a chalky candy like Neccos or Sweet Tarts. Will they all dissolve in the same way?

FLOATING CANDY LETTERS

When you eat a piece of candy, you might think about the delicious chocolate or fruity sweetness of the confection you're enjoying, but did you know that you are also eating an edible ink? Some of the familiar brands of candy we enjoy are stamped with letters. How do these stay on the surface of the candy, even when they're rattling around in their packages? Do these letters stay on even when we're eating them? With this experiment, you will investigate the properties of candy while taking a closer look at the labels on their surface.

MATERIALS NEEDED

A bag of M&Ms

A bag of Skittles

2 clear plastic cups

Water

PROCEDURE

1. Open your bags of candy, and make two piles: one for Skittles, and one for M&Ms.

2. Fill your plastic cups with water, and gently place 3 Skittles in one cup and 3 M&Ms in the other cup. Make sure they are both resting at the bottom with their letters facing up.

3. Observe the water as the candy coating begins to dissolve. What colors do you see in the water? Do the candies look the same as they dissolve?

4. After approximately 30 minutes, observe the surface of the water. What do you see? Can you see any individual letters floating up on the top of the water?

WHAT'S HAPPENING?

Some sweets are stamped with an edible ink. These inks will not dissolve in water. During this experiment, you observe the solubility of different parts of candy. While parts of the candy dissolve, other components float to the surface without dissolving, including the inks and waxy labels. This waxy coating that floats to the surface is what keeps the letters in place throughout the candy's packaging process.

TAKE IT FURTHER

Will all candies with a stamped label behave in this way? The next time you see Valentine's Day candy in the store, pick up a box of candy hearts to see if their labels react in the same way as Skittles or M&Ms. By experimenting with a variety of candies, you can test for the solubility of the sweet candy components to see which parts will dissolve in water, and which will not!

Marshmallow Animals GONE WILD

Every holiday season, grocery aisles are stocked with sweet treats, with everything from chocolate sweets to cute marshmallow-shaped chicks. With these experiments, you'll look at what those cute fluffy treats are made of and you'll conduct some sweet science along the way. You'll learn what makes these marshmallow chicks dissolve, how they react to changes in temperature, and you'll blast some radiation at them to blow them up!

MATERIALS NEEDED

Marshmallow chick candy

Ruler

Pen and paper

3 plastic cups

Vinegar

Water

Isopropyl alcohol

Permanent marker

Slotted spoon

Plate

Microwave

PROCEDURE

PART 1: LIQUID EFFECTS

1. Remove your marshmallow chicks from their packaging, and use your ruler to measure their length and width. While holding your candy, pay attention to what it feels like. What do you suppose it's made of?

2. Using your pen and paper, make a data table for your experiment. Your table should have three rows and four columns. Label each row with the name of your liquids, and each column: Day 1, Day 2, Day 3, and Day 4.

3. Fill each cup with one of your liquids, and use the permanent marker to label the cup with the liquid that is inside.

4. Place one marshmallow chick in each cup, and observe any changes that occur over the next five minutes. Record your observations in the first column of your data table.

5. Observe your marshmallow chicks over the next four days, and record any changes that you see. Make a prediction as to which liquid you think will cause the candy to dissolve, and see if, over time, your prediction is correct!

6. On the last day, use a slotted spoon to remove the candy from the cup and put it on a plate. Use your ruler to measure it and record any changes to the textures. Did any of the candies dissolve?

PART 2: HOT AND COLD

7. Place a new marshmallow chick on a microwave-safe plate, and put it in the microwave. Run the microwave on high power for 30 seconds, making sure to use your ruler to observe and record any changes to the candy.

8. Place another marshmallow chick on a plate, and put it in the freezer over night. Take it out the next morning and record any changes to the texture and size of the candy.

WHAT'S HAPPENING?

Marshmallow candies like these are made of fluffed-up sugar, water, and proteins in the form of gelatin. Gelatin is insoluble when it comes to water and other liquids, so you won't find any dissolving action in these marshmallow critters. However, they may readily absorb some of the liquids, causing them to grow larger. In the microwave, the molecules of the marshmallow chick are excited by the heat energy, and that causes the marshmallow candy to quickly expand!

LIGHTNING Life Savers

Some of the coolest and most unexpected experiments can come from the sweetest of treats, and this is no exception! Here, you'll be experimenting with physics and chemistry as you exert force on candy compounds that ignite a sense of curiosity. Grab a friend and get ready to light up your night with lightning Life Savers!

MATERIALS NEEDED

Wint-O-Green Life Savers candy

Pliers

Dark room

Mirror

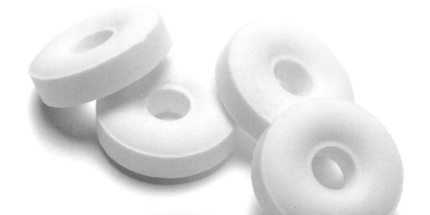

PROCEDURE

1. Unwrap a few Life Savers. Then grab your candy and a pair of pliers, and head into a dark room!

2. Spend a few minutes in the room as your eyes adjust to the lack of lighting.

3. Place a Life Savers candy vertically in your pliers, and then get to cracking! Repeat this a few times. What do you see?

4. You can also do this experiment in front of a mirror in a dark room. Place a Life Saver in your mouth and bite down, leaving your mouth open just enough to see the sparks fly!

WHAT'S HAPPENING?

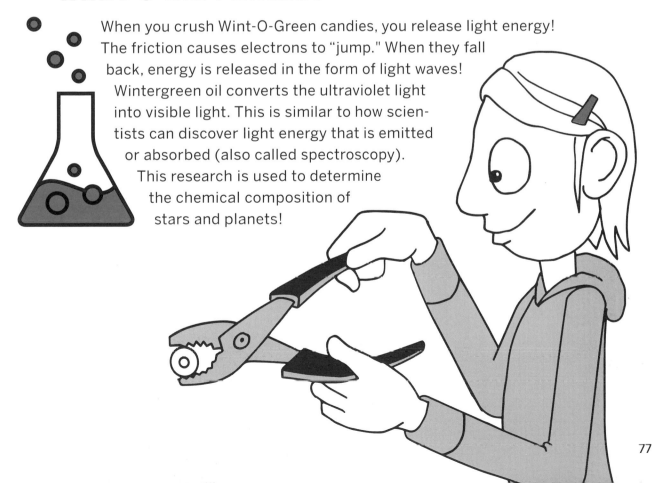

When you crush Wint-O-Green candies, you release light energy! The friction causes electrons to "jump." When they fall back, energy is released in the form of light waves! Wintergreen oil converts the ultraviolet light into visible light. This is similar to how scientists can discover light energy that is emitted or absorbed (also called spectroscopy). This research is used to determine the chemical composition of stars and planets!

SNIP

CHAPTER 6

SNIP

BUILDING REALISTIC BODY PARTS

GLUE

Build a Balloon Lung

Pay attention to how your chest expands when you breathe in a big gulp of air, then goes back inwards as you breathe out. Taking breaths like this is what keeps our body full of the oxygen that it needs to keep it functioning and to get rid of carbon dioxide waste. How do our lungs work like this every day without our even having to think about it? With this experiment, you'll use household materials to build a model of a lung so you can see how different muscles work together to open the lungs and breathe life-sustaining air into our bodies!

MATERIALS NEEDED

Plastic 1-liter bottle

Box cutter

2 latex balloons

Wide straw

Modeling clay

Rubber band

PROCEDURE

1. Remove the cap from your bottle. Using your box cutter, cut the 1-liter bottle in half, creating an even circle all the way around the bottle. Recycle the bottom half, and set aside the top half.

2. Pull one of the balloons 2-3 times to stretch it out, then tie it without inflating it. Cut the top of the balloon and stretch it around the bottom of the 1 liter bottle, so that the tied bottom is outside the bottle.

3. Take the straw and insert it into the neck of the other balloon, until about 1" of the straw is covered. Secure the balloon around the straw with a rubber band, making a tight seal.

4. Insert the balloon and the straw through the top of the soda bottle (where the cap was removed). Leave approximately 2-3" of space between the balloon and the bottom of the bottle. Seal the opening around the straw with modeling clay, creating an airtight seal.

5. Now you're going to imitate the movement of the diaphragm. Pull down gently on the tied end of the balloon secured to the bottom of the bottle, then push the tied end up into the bottle (without breaking the seal around the bottom of the bottle).

6. Repeat the pulling and pushing motion of the balloon, and observe the balloon that is sealed around the straw. Pretend that top balloon is one of your lungs. What do you notice about the balloon inside the bottle?

WHAT'S HAPPENING?

Every time you breathe in, your diaphragm contracts, moving downward. At the same time, the muscles connected to your rib cage pull your rib cage outward. Your lungs expand to fill this space. When you exhale, your diaphragm relaxes, rising into the chest cavity. This pushes your lungs back, deflating them. The balloon at the bottom of the bottle acts as the diaphragm, opening or deflating your lungs (the top balloon).

MAKE A
Skeleton Hand

Take a good look at your hands. Bend your fingers back and forth, and pay attention to the joints in your knuckles as you move. There is a lot involved in moving your hands! Under your skin, you have bones, muscles, nerves, and tendons, all working together to allow you to move and flex your fingers. But they don't just move by themselves: Something needs to pull them in the right direction. With this project, you'll be able to explore how tendons work to move your body, as you make your very own working model of a hand!

MATERIALS NEEDED

Pen

Craft foam

Scissors

Ruler

Paper straws

Double-sided sticky tape

Yarn

Wide-mouthed beads

Markers (optional)

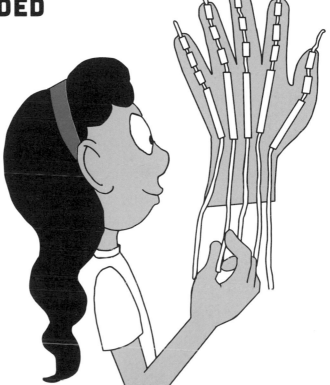

PROCEDURE

1. Begin by using your pen to trace your hand on a piece of craft foam, making sure to include your wrist. Then cut the shape out.

2. Cut 14 ½" pieces out of your straws. These will represent the bones in your fingers. Cut another five 2" pieces. These will represent the bones in your hand.

3. Tape your straw bones onto your foam hand. You will have three small ones on each finger, except for the thumb, which will have two. These small pieces will represent the short bones in between the knuckles in your fingers. Make sure to leave a nice space in between each piece of straw, so you can move your fingers later!

4. Leaving a ½" gap, line up the 5 larger straws below each bottom finger bone and tape them onto your hand. These will represent the long bones that go from your bottom knuckle down to your wrist.

5. Cut your yarn into five 12" lengths. Tie a bead at the end of each piece of yarn.

6. Thread each piece of yarn through your straw fingers leaving the beaded end at the tip of each finger. Make sure you follow the path so that one piece of yarn goes through all the bones in your thumb, index finger, middle finger, etc.

7. Finally, pull on each of the strings to move your fingers! Now you have a working articulated hand! For some additional creative fun, use your markers to decorate your hand with bracelets, rings, or nail colors.

WHAT'S HAPPENING?

Your fingers are all made of bones, muscles, and tendons. Your tendons are the strings that pull your muscles and your bones to move your fingers the way your brain wants them to move. The nerve cells within your tendons and muscles deliver electrical impulses sent from your brain. There are many pieces working together to keep a hand moving, and now you can see some of them in action.

EAT YOUR CAKE
AND DIGEST IT TOO

With this project, you will learn about the digestive system by building an anatomy model that is good enough to eat! Look at the digestive organ diagram provided or pull up your own diagram on your computer. Read the names of the organs and note their placement in your body. Now get ready to bake your own diagram! With some sweet confections as your ingredients, you'll get to have your cake and digest it too!

MATERIALS NEEDED

Cake mix and necessary ingredients to bake the cake

13" x 9" baking dish

Frosting

Diagram of human digestive system

Green, purple, and orange icing

Flat knife/icing spreader

Computer and printer

Scissors

Plastic wrap

Large and small marshmallows

Rope candy

Gummy worms

Index cards and markers

Toothpicks

Tape

PROCEDURE

1. Bake your cake according to the instructions on the box. Once it's done, let it cool for an hour and coat it in a thick, even layer of frosting.

2. Grab your diagram of the digestive system and discuss where you'll place your organs!

3. Print out a picture of the liver, the stomach, and the gall bladder or draw their shape and relative sizes onto paper. Cover your paper with plastic wrap and use your colored icing to trace the outline of the organ. Color in the shape with more icing and lay the frosting organ on a flat surface in your freezer for 15 minutes to solidify.

4. Now, create your model of the digestive system! Cut small marshmallows in half and use them for the teeth at the designated "top" of the cake. Cut your rope candy to a 5" length and use it for the esophagus. Refer to your diagram for the proper placement of each of your organs. When you're ready to use your icing organs, remove them from the freezer and place them on the cake where they belong.

5. Once you've built the organs, it's time to line intestines! Cut the large marshmallows in half and use them for the large intestines at the bottom of your diagram. Fill the opening inside with gummy worms for the small intestines.

6. Once you've finished building the digestive system, it's time to label your anatomy cake! Cut the index cards into small strips, and write the names of the organs on them. Tape the labels to the toothpicks and put them in their proper places. Have a science party and share your diagram with others before slicing and eating it!

WHAT'S HAPPENING?

You have the whole digestive system on your cake! Food gets ground up by your teeth, travels down to your stomach where it turns into liquid, then exits your body through your intestines!

The BIG Squeeze: Intestines at Work

When we take a bite of food, our mouths immediately kick off the process of digestion with mashing, chewing, and swallowing. Then the food heads down the esophagus and into the stomach, where strong acids break down food into a soupy mixture. In this experiment, you'll create a model of the digestive system to see the process of digestion in action. All you'll need are some nylon stockings and some common kitchen ingredients, and you're well on your way to discovering the sticky, slimy, and messy process carried out in the digestive system.

MATERIALS NEEDED

Soft or crumbly food
(peanut butter sandwich or crackers)

Scissors

1 pair of nylon stockings

Zip-closed freezer bag

½ cup water

½ cup orange juice

Shallow pan

Paper towels

PROCEDURE

1. Make yourself some lunch! A peanut butter sandwich works well for this experiment, but you can also use crackers, cheese, or any other soft food.

2. Use your scissors to cut away one of the legs from the nylon stockings. Keep the toe intact, leaving you with an opening near the top and a closed bottom.

3. Take your peanut butter sandwich and break it up into tiny pieces. This will mimic the process of chewing that breaks your food down. Put the pieces into the plastic bag and add the water. This will act as the saliva, further breaking down your food.

4. Add the orange juice to the bag, simulating the hydrochloric stomach acids that work to break down your food. Continue mashing your food as your hands mimic the muscles in your stomach, pushing your food around as it interacts with the acid inside.

5. Now you should have a soupy mess of digestion! Hold the nylon tube over the pan, and pour your liquid into the opening. Start squeezing the liquid through the nylon, mimicking the food traveling through the small intestine. You'll see a ton of watery material drain out of the nylon. This would be the nutrient-rich material that is absorbed through the small intestine.

6. Once you've squeezed the water out, cut open the end of the nylon. As most of the liquid has been absorbed by the small intestine, you will see a solid mass of digested food. Now it's time to work through the large intestine.

7. Grab your paper towels, and press firmly into the solid material. The paper towels are now acting as the large intestine, absorbing the rest of the moisture out of your food substance. Once the rest of the water is absorbed, the final product is a solid pile of waste. This would exit your body as it departs from the digestive system through the colon and out of your body!

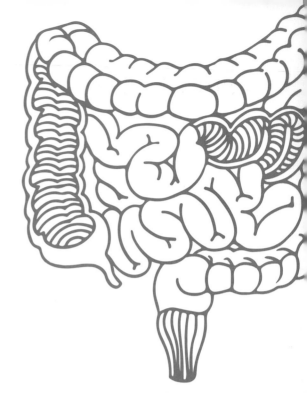

WHAT'S HAPPENING?

Digestion is an exciting process that involves a large number of organs inside your body! Once your food is pushed into your stomach, your stomach muscles churn the food about, while highly acidic compounds called gastric acids break apart the proteins and fats in your food. The food then goes through the small intestine.

Once your food has traveled through your small intestine, it makes its way through the large intestine. From here, it will be stored until it can be eliminated from your body as waste (poop).

TAKE IT FURTHER

Here you can experiment with different acids to see which ones will break down your food the fastest. Try vinegar, orange juice, or soda, and compare the results! You can also experiment with the amount of time your food is worked through your intestines. If you only pull a small amount of water from the nylon, what kind of waste is left behind? Is it more solid, or does it contain more liquid?

A Bloody-Good HEART PUMP

The heart works hard every second of every day to keep your body going. The heart brings oxygen to your body and carries carbon dioxide waste out of your body through your lungs. The human heart is divided into right and left sides, and each side has a ventricle and an atrium. One side of your heart fills with oxygen-rich blood to deliver to your bloodstream. The other side pumps blood carrying CO_2 to your lungs so it can be exhaled. You can build a model to see how this works! All it takes is a few household materials.

MATERIALS NEEDED

Wide-mouthed jar

Water

Large shallow pan or sink

Red food coloring

Balloon

Scissors

Tape

2 flexible straws

PROCEDURE

1. Fill the jar halfway with water, then set the jar in the shallow pan or the sink. Then add red food coloring to resemble blood.

2. Cut the neck off the balloon, right where it starts to widen. Set the neck piece aside and stretch your balloon to soften the rubber.

3. Stretch the balloon around the rim of your jar. Pull the balloon down around the jar as far as you can, leaving a smooth, flat surface over the top of your container.

4. Use the scissors to make two very small holes in center of the balloon, approximately 1" apart. The holes should only be large enough to fit the straws through, but small enough to seal around the straw. If there is any space between the balloon and the straw, seal it with tape to make it airtight.

5. Slide a straw into each hole, bendy-side up. The flexible top of the straws should be sticking up out of the jar.

6. Take the neck of the balloon that you set aside and use it to seal the open top of one of the straws. Use tape to secure it around the straw, to make sure that no air can pass through it. Bend the other straw downward.

7. Use your hand to start pushing gently down on the jar's balloon seal until water start to pump out of your straw.

WHAT'S HAPPENING?

The neck of the balloon over one of the straws acts as a valve, blocking any of your blood from flowing back through the "plumbing system." The other straw allows blood flow to pass through. This mimics the dual-action pumping of the heart. When we breathe air into our lungs, it is cycled through our blood by our heart. The carbon dioxide waste that is left behind is pushed back through our heart and out of our lungs.

Crafting the HUMAN HEART

Place your hand on your chest and feel the rhythm of your heart. As your heart beats, it is pumping blood through your entire body! This blood carries oxygen to your cells, it provides a highway for the immune system to attack invading viruses, and it carries carbon dioxide waste out of your body. Your heart has a big job, but do you know what it looks like? With this project, you'll learn all about how the heart looks and what it does and you'll make your very own anatomically correct model!

MATERIALS NEEDED

Thick, milkshake straws

Scissors

Aluminum foil

Toothpicks

Hot glue gun

Rolling pin

Red and blue modeling clay

Pipe cleaners

Red crepe paper

*Heart diagram, if needed

PROCEDURE

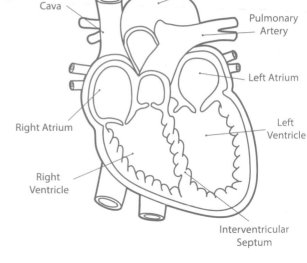

1. Cut your milkshake straws into small artery pieces: You will need 5 ½" pieces, three 1" pieces, and two 2" pieces. Set them aside.

2. Use the aluminum foil to make two small balls and one medium-sized ball. Two should be the size of a golf ball and one should be the size of a tennis ball.

3. Firmly press 3 toothpicks into the top-left side of the larger ball. Use the hot glue to secure the toothpicks in place. Position one of the smaller foil balls onto the picks, spearing it into place. Repeat the toothpick procedure on the top-right side of the larger ball. Place the other small foil ball onto the toothpicks.

4. Cover the rolling pin with aluminum foil, so that the clay will not stick to it. Then use your rolling pin to roll flat some sections of red clay. Use this clay to cover the entire foil model you have made (not each individual ball). Cover your foil pieces with clay and shape it until it begins to look like a human heart. (Use the illustrations above and at left to guide you as you craft.)

5. Once you're finished with the shape of the heart, it's time to start on the aorta. Hold 6 pipe cleaners tightly together, then bend them in half so that they fold in half. Use the hot glue to secure the ends in place so they do not pop open.

6. Bend the folded pipe cleaners into a U-shape. Wind the crepe paper around the pipe cleaners until they are fully covered. Use hot glue to secure the paper in place.

7. Stick 3 toothpicks on one end of the U-shaped pipe cleaners. Glue them in place and stick the aorta into the top of the heart, at the center of the bend. Bend the U-shape so that it ends behind the right side of the heart and glue it into place.

8. Now it's time to work on the pulmonary trunk. Take 3 pipe cleaners and bend them in half so they fold in on each other. Use hot glue to secure the ends together. Bend the pipe cleaners so that they have a slight curve. Then use the red crepe paper to cover the pipe cleaners, and glue the paper into place.

9. Stick 3 toothpicks in one end of the pulmonary trunk. Firmly press the toothpicks into the top left side of the heart, using hot glue to secure them in place. Bend the pulmonary trunk so that it hugs the aorta, and bends slightly behind it. Use glue to secure one of the ½" pieces of straw to the end.

10. For the pulmonary arteries, take 2 pipe cleaners and bend them together as you did for the aorta and pulmonary trunk, using glue to secure the ends together. Wrap them with crepe paper and use glue to secure it in place. Thread this through the loop of the aorta and behind the pulmonary trunk. Use your glue to secure it in place, then use glue to attach two ½" pieces of straw to each end, making a V-shape.

11. Now, it's time to connect the last of your arteries. The 1" pieces should be spaced evenly apart, so they stick out along the top of the aorta. Finally, the 2" pieces should stick out of the right side of the heart.

12. Finally, roll out some blue clay into thin strips, and line the bottom of your heart with some posterior veins.

Now you're finished with your very own anatomical model of the human heart! Enjoy admiring your creative handiwork, and place it in a place where you can display it proudly.

WHAT'S HAPPENING?

The heart is divided into two halves, with each half divided into two sections. The top chambers consist of the left and right atria, where oxygenated blood from the lungs, or deoxygenated blood returning from the body, is collected. As we breathe out the carbon dioxide waste and inhale fresh oxygen rich air, the blood travels back to the left side of the heart to begin the process of circulation all over again!

SEE

CHAPTER 7

SNIFF

TEST YOUR SENSES

SLURP

Make a FROZEN LENS

Look at your surroundings. What do you see? If you look off into the distance, do you see a building, a tree, or a hill? Observe the clouds, then look down at your feet. Your eyes are moving around and adjusting to distances in the matter of seconds, allowing you to focus and see what's in front of you! How do our eyes adjust to different settings? The answer has to do with lenses, and with this experiment, you'll learn how they work and also experiment with a variety of light-bending materials.

MATERIALS NEEDED

Small cup of water

Dime

Quarter

Penny

Tennis ball

Box cutter

Vegetable oil

Small glass of distilled water

Magazine

PROCEDURE

1. Dip your finger in a small cup of water. Place a few drops of water onto your coins.

2. As you look through the water and onto the surface of your coins, what do you see? Does the water magnify the writing on the back of the coins?

3. Now we're going to use water to make a bigger lens, and this time, you'll make it out of ice. Grab the tennis ball, and use the box cutter to carefully cut it in half.

4. Use your finger to rub a light coating of vegetable oil on the inside of the tennis ball half. Then set the tennis ball in the small glass, so that it just fits on the top and forms a sort of bowl.

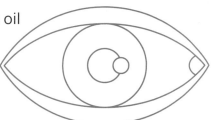

5. Fill the tennis ball with distilled water until it just reaches the brim.

6. Place the glass and tennis ball in the freezer. Do not disturb the water until it is fully frozen. However, continue to check on the water until it has completely frozen through. If it stays in the freezer for too long, it may become cloudy, which can hinder its ability to magnify.

7. Once the water is completely frozen through, carefully pop it out of the tennis ball. Use your hands and fingers to smooth over any rough edges on the flat side of the ice.

8. Now you have an ice lens! It's not a perfect lens, as smooth glass is much clearer than ice, and the curvature of the ice lens is too great for clear magnification. However, you can use it to read letters on your magazine, and see pictures up close.

WHAT'S HAPPENING?

When light passes through the curved surface of our eye, it bends! This is called refraction and it allows us to see sharp images. The ice lens is thicker in the middle and thinner on the outer edges, just like the one in each of your eyes. This shape helps to refract light and focus it to a single point to produce a clear image.

Colorblind
TASTE TEST

Think about what you had for lunch. What were the colors on your plate? There is a lot that goes into eating our food, beyond smell and taste. Sight plays a big part in what we eat, so we can identify familiar foods, as well as foods we enjoy. What do you think would happen if you changed the colors of your foods? Would you still enjoy them? This experiment looks at how color and sight affect our perception of foods. So fill a plate, grab some food coloring, and prepare to let your eyes take the lead!

MATERIALS NEEDED

6 small plastic cups

A favorite fruit
(try sliced apples, pineapple, peaches, or banana)

Red and green food coloring

A favorite side dish
(mashed potatoes, macaroni and cheese, or yogurt works well!)

Blindfold

A partner

A glass of water

Marker

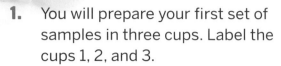

PROCEDURE

1. You will prepare your first set of samples in three cups. Label the cups 1, 2, and 3.

2. Fill your cups with equal amounts of the same fruit. In cup 1, add a couple of drops of red food coloring, and stir to coat your fruit evenly. In cup 2, add a couple of drops of green food coloring, and stir to coat the fruit evenly. Leave cup 3 alone as it will be your control.

3. Prepare your second set of samples, following the same procedure. Place equal amounts of the same side-dish food in each cup, and evenly coat two of them with red and green food coloring.

4. Sit your partner down at a table, and blindfold her. Go through your first set of samples, giving her a spoonful from each cup. Give her time to slowly savor each bite, and offer a drink of water between samples if needed. When finished, ask her (while still blindfolded), which sample she liked best. Record the answers.

5. Repeat the process with your second set of samples. Record her preference.

6. Now, lift the blindfold. Ask her which sample she would prefer to eat from if given the choice. Record this answer next to the previous answers. Show her which one she preferred while blindfolded, and see how it compares to when she was looking at the food!

WHAT'S HAPPENING?

Does sight affect your ability to taste your food? Being able to see our food gives us important clues as to its safety. Some foods that look green may have gone bad, or have spoiled. Other foods may give us visual clues as to whether they might be poisonous or harmful to us. Visual cues are important, as our brain records this information, letting us know which foods are safe and palatable.

SOUND
Gun Science

Did you know that sound moves through the air in waves? You may not be able to see the waves, but you can see their effect on the environment. In this experiment, you'll build a "sound gun" that you can use to propel objects with the power of sound! All it takes are some household materials, and you're well on your way to drumming your way through the visual aspects of sound.

MATERIALS NEEDED

Paper towel roll

Scissors

Plastic wrap

Rubber band

Pencil

Cardstock

Thumbtack

Tape

Bowl

Sand

Candle

Matches or lighter
(with help from an adult)

Construction paper

PROCEDURE

1. Cut the paper towel roll in half, then cover one end of the paper towel roll with plastic wrap. Pull it tight to create a flat surface, and then use the rubber band to secure it in place.

2. Take the other end of the paper towel roll and use it to trace a circle onto the card stock. Use the thumbtack to poke a small hole in the center of the circle. Then cut out the circle and place it over the uncovered end of the paper towel roll and use tape to secure it in place.

3. Fill a small bowl with sand, then place a candle in the center and light it. Hold the sound gun so that the small hole in the cardstock is about 1" away from the flame. Tap the plastic-wrapped end with your fingers, and observe what happens with the flame!

WHAT'S HAPPENING?

When something makes noise, it creates small vibrations that move through the air in the form of sound waves. These waves reach our ear and vibrate the tiny bones of the inner ear. This triggers nerve responses in our brain that let us know that we are hearing a specific sound. You are demonstrating this when you tap your sound gun. The sound waves that move through the tube are focused through a small hole and projected onto your paper and candle.

TAKE IT FURTHER

Here's a fun variation: Cover a small bowl with a tight layer of plastic wrap. Use a rubber band to secure it around the sides. Place a few grains of rice in the middle of the plastic. Then take a cooking pot and a wooden spoon, and bang on the pot with the spoon right next to the rice. What do you notice?

The OUCH Sensitivity Test

We use our sense of touch to navigate everything, from what clothes to wear, to how to drive, to how to hold things in our hand. Our sense of touch is derived from nerves all over our body, and it's interpreted by signals sent to and from our brain. Just how sensitive are those nerves? Can we feel the same things with various parts of our body? With this experiment, you'll be able to determine where humans are most sensitive to touch.

MATERIALS NEEDED

Compass

Pencil

Cardboard

Two colored markers

Scissors

Toothpicks

Blindfold

A partner

PROCEDURE

1. Use your compass to draw a 3 ½" circle on your cardboard. Then draw a smaller circle inside of that, and another circle in the middle. Each circle should be ½" apart from the other.

2. Use your markers to color in the outer and inner circles. These will be your sensitivity zones. Use your scissors to cut around the outer edge, so you have a large circle with different colored circles inside of it.

3. Take 4 toothpicks and stick them into the center circle, making sure they are all of equal lengths. Then blindfold your partner, and get to testing!

4. Without informing your partner of where you'll be testing, begin first on the arm. Lightly touch all four tips of the toothpicks to your partner's bare arm, and ask how many toothpicks can be felt.

5. Next, try placing the toothpicks on the palm of your partner's hand. How many toothpicks can be felt in this location?

6. Try your partner's back, and ask if your partner can determine how many toothpicks are on the end of the circle.

7. Finally, touch the toothpicks to your partner's fingertips. How many toothpicks can be felt in this location?

8. Continue this experiment in different parts of the body. Try placing the toothpicks onto your partner's tongue, the back of her arm, her leg, on her stomach, and on her feet. Try moving all of the toothpicks from the center circle to one of the outer circles and see how that changes the results.

9. Have your partner pick a different number of toothpicks, and repeat the experiment on you. Can you tell how many toothpicks are touching you at any given point?

WHAT'S HAPPENING?

When the toothpick touches our skin, the touch receptors send an electrical impulse to our brain to help us understand what we're feeling. Areas like our fingertips and tongue have more receptors than our arms and back, so they are able to provide more detailed information to our brain.

The Scent DETECTIVE Game

Can you smell a book by its cover?

Can you tell if a book has been opened, merely by smelling it? We generally rely on our sense of sight to see if something is amiss, but we can use our sense of smell too! Take your sense of smell for a spin and put your detective skills to the test! By dampening your other senses, you can pay close attention to the olfactory cells in your nose to decipher clues as to who has been messing with your library.

MATERIALS NEEDED

Books on a bookshelf

Blindfold

A partner

PROCEDURE

PART 1: TRACK THE SCENT

1. With your partner in another room, choose a selection of 5 books. (Make sure they are all right next to each other!)

2. Take one book off the shelf and rub your hands all over it. Make sure you only touch one book. When you are finished, put the book back in its place on the bookshelf.

3. Call your partner in the room and point to the selection of books. One by one, have your partner pull each book off the bookshelf and smell it. Can your partner tell which book you have handled?

4. Trade places! Will you be able to tell which book your partner has touched?

PART 2: AN OPEN-AND-SHUT CASE

There is a distinct smell that books have. The paper, the ink, the binding, the glue—all these things culminate into a specific "book smell." Can you tell if the seal of a closed book has been opened?

5. With your partner in another room, choose another selection of 5 books, making sure they are all next to each other on a bookshelf.

6. Open a book in the middle and flip through the pages a few times. Close the book and put it back in its place on the library shelf.

7. Call your partner into the room and point to the selection of books. One by one, have your partner pull each book off the bookshelf and smell it. Can your partner tell which book has just been opened?

8. Trade places! Will you be able to tell which book your partner has touched?

WHAT'S HAPPENING?

As we breathe in, tiny particles enter our nose. They come in contact with olfactory neurons and fire off an electrical impulse. The impulse is sent to our brain, identifying the smell. Here, you identify a difference in dust particles and detect odor from your partner's hands to figure out which books are disturbed during your tests.

SMELL IT,
Don't Tell It

Can you identify what's around you, using only your sense of smell? What if you had food on your plate that was completely inedible—or worse, had gone bad? Would you be able to tell without looking at it? Can you differentiate between an actual orange and an orange-scented candle? When you aren't able to use one of your senses, you allow some of the other senses to come alive. Grab some food, some shoes, and some crazy household items, and discover just how powerful your sense of smell can be with this experiment!

MATERIALS NEEDED

Variety of edible items
(apples, yogurt,
crackers, etc.)

Variety of inedible items
(air freshener spray, shoe,
book, etc.)

Small containers
to hold your items

Paper

Pen

Partner

Blindfold

PROCEDURE

1. Have your partner stay in another room (or another area—no peeking!) while you fill your containers with your test items. We used a lemon, an apple, yogurt, an orange, air freshener spray, a shoe, kettle corn, soap, vanilla, and an onion. Make sure to mix them up so there is not a predictable order of smells.

2. On your paper, number and label the test items. Make a chart labeled Item/Edible/Inedible/Identified.

3. Blindfold your partner and slowly guide him/her to the table. See if your partner can identify any smells along the way.

4. Sit your partner down and begin testing! One by one, raise each dish under your partner's nose. Ask whether the item is edible or inedible, as well as whether he/she can identify what the smell is.

5. Swap in new items and see if your partner can identify them. Switch roles and have your partner find items to test your sense of smell. Whose nose "knows" the most?

WHAT'S HAPPENING?

Our sense of smell provides an important evolutionary advantage: being able to distinguish between edible foods and substances that could potentially harm us.

Our noses pick up tiny particles floating around the air. These particles attach themselves to nose receptors called olfactory neurons. Once these receptors are triggered, impulses are sent to your brain, identifying the smell and triggering the proper response. These responses can range from a sense of urgency (fire danger), to pleasant feelings, to hunger!

GLOP

CHAPTER 8

STRETCH

ADVENTURES IN .SLIME

SPLAT

IT'S ALIVE:
The Properties of
SLIME

If you were to plunge your hand into a glob of slime, what you do expect would happen? You might assume that your hand would be covered in a sticky substance, since you just soaked it in a liquid! Surprisingly, this isn't always the case; there are some substances that do not behave as expected. We call them non-Newtonian fluids, and they have the unique ability to take on the characteristics of a liquid and a solid at the same time. With this project, you will be explore solids and liquids and the strange behavior of non-Newtonian fluids.

MATERIALS NEEDED

2 cups of cornstarch

1 cup of water

Bowl

Paper towels

PROCEDURE

1. Pour 1 cup of water into a large bowl. Add ½ cup of cornstarch at a time, and stir it in to thoroughly combine the mixture.

2. As you get closer to 2 cups of cornstarch, you will find the substance more difficult to mix. Now it's time to get your hands dirty and start getting messy! Use your hands to combine the mixture until the substance feels like a solid when you grasp it tightly, and a liquid when you run your fingers slowly through it.

3. Allow the mixture to settle into the bowl. Once it forms an even layer, punch your hand into it! This would be a great time to invite a friend over to punch a bowl of slime, super fast and super hard!

4. Now take your hands and slowly rake them through the mixture. What do you feel? Is it any different than when you were punching the mixture? Try to scoop some up in your hand and make a tight fist. When you unfurl your fingers, what do you see?

5. Clean up: Cornstarch and water cleans up very easily with soap and water. However, if you have large amounts of it, it's best to discard it into the trash rather than pour it through your drain. It will maintain its non-Newtonian properties in your pipes as well, and you don't want the pipes clogging up as the forces of water exert pressure on them!

WHAT'S HAPPENING?

Cornstarch and water creates a non-Newtonian fluid. This means that instead of behaving like a liquid or a solid, it can behave as both! Molecules have a consistent structure once they've combined. Liquid molecules tend to be loosely organized, while molecules in a solid object tend to be locked in place. In a non-Newtonian fluid, molecules will act as liquid until a force is applied, in which case they will quickly lock up as if they were a solid!

BOUNCING POLYMER PUTTY

What's better than a slime recipe that you can stretch, bounce, and play with as you experiment your way through sticky, slimy polymers? With just a few household ingredients, you can experiment with polymers in a way that leaves you with a fun toy you can play with for days to come!

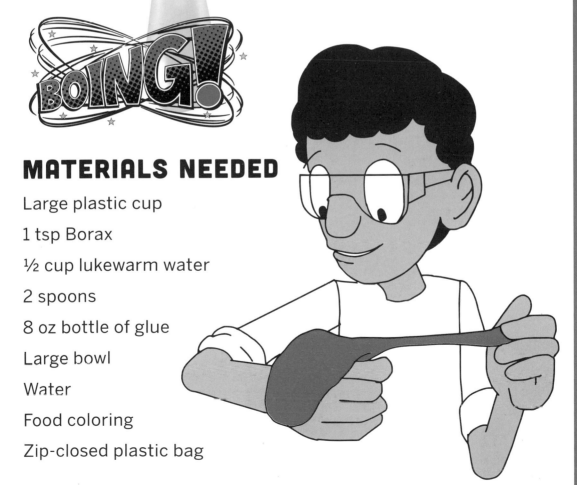

MATERIALS NEEDED

Large plastic cup

1 tsp Borax

½ cup lukewarm water

2 spoons

8 oz bottle of glue

Large bowl

Water

Food coloring

Zip-closed plastic bag

PROCEDURE

1. In the plastic cup, mix one teaspoon of Borax with ½ cup of lukewarm water, stirring thoroughly to combine. Leave your spoon in the cup and set the mixture to the side.

2. Empty your bottle of glue into a large bowl, then fill the bottle of glue with water and swirl it around. Empty the water into the bowl of glue and use your second spoon to thoroughly stir the glue-and-water mixture until it has completely combined.

3. Add your desired color of food coloring to your glue-and-water mixture. Stir the coloring in until it is thoroughly combined.

4. Use your Borax spoon to spoon the Borax-and-water mixture into your glue and water solution. Continue stirring as you add the Borax into your mixture.

5. Once the solution becomes slimy and sticky, keep stirring until the slime begins to pull away from the sides of the bowl. Then take it out and knead it with your hands until it forms a consistency that is similar to Silly Putty. Time to play! When you're finished playing with your putty, place it in a plastic zip-closed bag until you're ready to take it out and play with it again.

WHAT'S HAPPENING?

Glue is made of polymers, which are long chains of the same type of molecule linked together. Once you add the Borax, it immediately starts connecting to these chains in every direction. When these polymer chains link up to the Borax, you get a strong bond of sticky, bouncy putty!

TAKE IT FURTHER

Use clear glue and green food coloring to create putty that looks like boogers and will seriously gross out your friends! Or get artsy and add glitter, small toys, and even beads to your putty to create a sensory masterpiece of sticky fun!

Water Bead OSMOSIS

Have you ever grown a "dinosaur" or a "snake" toy in water? How do these toys grow from such a small size? In this experiment, you'll discover how these toys work by growing and experimenting with water beads. Water beads are usually used in floral arrangements and gardening supplies, but you can use them to experiment with polymers as you learn and play through chemistry. Gather a few simple items and you're well on your way to understanding osmosis, absorption, and the wonderful world of polymers!

MATERIALS NEEDED

2 clear glasses

2 cups water

¼ tsp salt

Spoon

Water beads/water marbles

Small strainer

2 small bowls

111

PROCEDURE

1. Fill both glasses with 1 cup of water. In one of the cups, add ¼ tsp of salt and stir to thoroughly combine.

2. Add ½ tsp of water beads to each cup, and leave them in a place where they will be undisturbed for three hours.

3. Periodically check in on your water beads to see how they are growing. Are there any differences in the growth rates in each glass?

4. Leave the beads for 24 hours, then use the spoon to scoop them out and drain them using the strainer. Leave the water in the glasses. Place the beads into two separate bowls: one for salt water beads, and the other for the plain water beads.

5. Measure the amount of water that is left behind in each glass. Is there a difference in the amounts? Is there a difference in the size of the beads you gathered from your cups?

WHAT'S HAPPENING?

The water beads are made up of large molecular chains called polymers. Polymers occur naturally in the world as bones, DNA, leather, silk, and wool. This polymer absorbs water! The polymers absorb the salt water, too, but at a different rate. This is because the salt water passes through the membrane of the water bead and wants to equalize the inside of the water bead with the outside, creating an equilibrium.

TAKE IT FURTHER

Experiment with different solutions and your water beads! Would you get the same effect with sugar water? You can also try juices, or water with food coloring to see if the beads absorb the same amount.

The Science of STICKINESS

What's better than a science experiment that leaves you sticky, slimy, and gooey afterwards? With this experiment, you'll study the chemistry of polymers and slime, and come up with the perfect slime recipe. All you need are some school supplies and laundry detergent, and you're ready to go! Roll up your sleeves and prepare to find yourself in a sticky situation!

MATERIALS NEEDED

¼ cup of clear school glue

¼ cup of water

Large plastic cup

Food coloring

¼ cup of liquid starch
(found in the laundry aisle)

Large bowl

Plastic spoon

Plastic bag

PROCEDURE

1. Pour the glue and water into one of the large cups and stir for approximately one minute, to ensure that they are thoroughly combined.

2. Add several drops of food coloring to the glue-and-water mixture and stir to combine.

3. Pour the liquid starch into a glass bowl, then pour your glue-and-water mixture into the starch. Grab your plastic spoon and start stirring!

4. You should notice your starch immediately begin to thicken as the glue and water binds to the starch. Continue stirring for a couple of minutes until it thickens enough to peel away from the edges. Then take it out and play with it!

5. The more you play with this slime, the stickier it gets! When you are finished playing with it, seal it inside your plastic bag so you can use it another time.

WHAT'S HAPPENING?

Everything is made up of atoms, which link together into molecules. These molecules also form bigger things and sometimes form long chains. The glue in this demonstration consists of long pieces of polymer chains. When you add the starch to your glue-and-water mixture, it grabs several of these chains and cross-links them together. This makes them immediately bond into a strong, flexible polymer that you can play with!

FIZZ

CHAPTER 9

BUBBLE

ALL THINGS FUN AND GASSY

POP

ERUPTING Soda Geysers

What happens when you combine a tight space, a lot of pressure, and some explosive chemistry? You get a gushing geyser right in your own backyard! With this classic experiment, you can create just the right conditions for an explosive fountain of soda, and you might just satisfy your sweet tooth at the same time! All you'll need is a bottle of soda, a package of Mentos, and you're well on your way to some high-pressure science!

MATERIALS NEEDED

A piece of paper

2-liter bottle of diet soda

A roll of Mentos candy

Index card

A flat surface outside that you will be able to rinse with the hose

PROCEDURE

1. Take the piece of paper and roll it into a tube that is approximately ½" in diameter. Make sure it is just wide enough to fit your Mentos.

2. Head outside, unscrew the cap from the bottle of diet soda, and place the bottle down on a flat surface. Place the index card over the opening of the soda bottle.

3. Place your paper tube upright on top of the index card, directly over the opening of the soda bottle. Open the Mentos and drop them one at a time into your tube. You may need to straighten them out as you go along, as you want them resting flat, one on top of the other.

4. Remove the index card to allow all of the Mentos to drop into the soda at once, and then get out of the way. It's about to get messy!

WHAT'S HAPPENING?

Mentos contains a lot of little dents in the candy shell. When you drop them into the soda, these pores allow the carbon dioxide bubbles in the soda to form on them and build up quickly. Once these bubbles start forming, they will not stop until all the carbon dioxide is released. This creates a lot of pressure in the bottle, which leads to the fantastic KABOOM you see when it erupts!

TAKE IT FURTHER

Try this experiment with a variety of sodas to see which varieties are the best for erupting geysers. Try diet sodas, regular, caffeinated, non-caffeinated soda, and carbonated water. You can also try gently placing the Mentos in a cup of soda to see if you still get the eruption that occurs when the candies are rapidly dropped in place!

Bubbling Wonders
LAVA LAMP

Alka-Seltzer is a common effervescent used to relieve an upset stomach and acid indigestion. You can also use it to create a fantastic fizzing, bubbling, chemical reaction! With this experiment, you can create a mesmerizing lava lamp right in your kitchen! All you need is oil, water, and some effervescent (Alka-Seltzer) tablets to create a fun and psychedelic bit of kitchen chemistry.

MATERIALS NEEDED

¾ cup of water

Funnel

A clean 1-liter bottle

Vegetable oil

Food coloring

1 or 2 effervescent tablets

118

PROCEDURE

1. Pour ¾ cup of water through the funnel and into the water bottle. Then use the funnel to fill the bottle with vegetable oil until it almost reaches the top. Leave about 2" from the top of the oil to the top of the bottle.

2. Allow the oil and water to settle into their respective layers. Oil is less dense than water, so it will eventually settle on top of the water.

3. Drop 10-20 drops of food coloring into the bottle. Watch as it falls through the oil and collects into a layer on the bottom of the oil. Once it sinks through the water, pay attention to the difference in how the food coloring behaves in the two substances!

4. Break your effervescent tablets in half and drop each of them into the bottle, one piece at a time. Sit back and enjoy the reaction!

WHAT'S HAPPENING?

Food coloring is made up mostly of water, and water has surface tension, meaning it clings to itself. Oil, however, is hydrophobic, meaning it that it doesn't mix well with water. The atoms that make up the outer layer of the food coloring won't bond with the oil. When you drop the effervescent tablets into the water, it begins to react, resulting in a lot of carbon dioxide gas. These gas bubbles rise to the surface, but once they hit the oil layer, the dense water sinks back down again, creating a lava lamp of moving bubbles!

TAKE IT FURTHER

Try this experiment with hot water as well as cold water. Do the bubbles expand at the same rate? What if you used a different oil? What would happen if you left the cap on while you ran your lava lamp? You can make this into a true lava lamp by shining a light under it as you watch the chemical reaction! Keep the cap closed when your lamp is not in use.

FIZZING VOLCANOES

When we think of fun science experiments, we often imagine bubbling, fizzing concoctions that react together to create a mess of fun and learning.

This is one of those! With this experiment, you'll explore one of the most memorable chemistry demonstrations: the baking soda and vinegar volcano. Why do these substances react together to create this foamy, mess of science? To find out, grab some baking soda and vinegar, and get ready to fizz your way through chemistry!

MATERIALS NEEDED

Rolling pin

Modeling clay

Paper or plastic cup

Shallow baking dish

Baking soda

Small cup

Vinegar

Red food coloring

PROCEDURE

1. Use the rolling pin to flatten a block of modeling clay into a long, wide strip.

2. Place your paper cup on its side at one end of your clay. Roll the clay around the cup until it is covered on all sides. This is the crater for your volcano!

3. Add additional clay if desired and shape the crater into a volcano, making sure no clay covers the opening of the volcano.

4. Place your volcano in the baking dish and drop a tablespoon of baking soda into the paper cup crater.

5. Pour some vinegar into another cup, and use 5-10 drops of food coloring to create a rich red color, swirling it to combine.

6. Now, you're ready for a fizzing volcano explosion! Pour the vinegar onto the baking soda inside your volcano and observe the reaction!

WHAT'S HAPPENING?

Some liquids and solids can combine and create a gas! How does that happen? Vinegar is an acid. When acids and bases interact, protons are exchanged, changing the structure of these molecules. What's left behind is a mixture of water and carbon dioxide gas. This is what causes the fizzing bubbles in your volcano. As the pressure builds from bubbling gases, the liquid rises higher and higher until it spills out over the top of your volcano!

TAKE IT FURTHER

Next time, add some dish soap to the baking soda in the crater of the volcano. What happens to the bubbles when you create your chemical reaction? You can also experiment with other acids, like orange juice and apple juice (in place of the vinegar).

Color-Changing EXPLOSIONS

If you've ever played with baking soda and vinegar, you know these materials can react in a really exciting way. With this experiment, you'll explore the concept of acids and bases while creating a colorful tower of foaming density. You'll layer liquids on top of each other and, with the power of chemistry, you'll watch the colors of your ingredients change right before your eyes!

MATERIALS NEEDED

1 cup finely chopped red cabbage

Heat-resistant bowl

Water

Strainer

Pitcher

Narrow glass vase

Metal baking tray

Small cup

Spoon

Baking soda

Vinegar

PROCEDURE

1. Place 1 cup of finely chopped red cabbage in the heat-resistant bowl. Cover the cabbage with hot water and let it stand for approximately 10 minutes, until the water turns to a dark blue.

2. Pour the cabbage water through a strainer and into the pitcher. Discard the solid cabbage pieces.

3. Add one cup of water to the cabbage water to dilute the pigmentation. Now, you've got a pH indicator! Fill your glass vase halfway with indicator solution, and set it in the middle of your baking tray.

4. In the small cup, mix 2 tablespoons of baking soda with ½ cup of water. Stir to combine the mixture, then pour it into your indicator solution. Observe the color change as the baking soda interacts with the indicator.

5. Pour a small amount of vinegar into the indicator solution. Stand back and watch as the baking soda and vinegar react and the solution fizzes over. After it bubbles out, observe the layers of color in your column.

6. Add more baking soda to your solution. Can you change the color from red to blue or purple? Can you bring it back to red again?

WHAT'S HAPPENING?

When you soak cabbage leaves in water, you create an indicator solution, a liquid that can change color in the presence of an acid or a base! This is due to the special pigments called anthocyanins that are found within the cabbage leaves. They change from pink to red in the presence of an acid, or blue to yellow with a base. These colors form layers when materials of different densities are added to the solution.

ELEPHANT Toothpaste

With this experiment, you'll use chemistry to create elephant toothpaste, a foamy substance that looks like an elephant might use it to brush its teeth! This chemical reaction releases heat, fizz, and a lot of oozing foam in an exothermic reaction. Get your gloves, grab some strong hydrogen peroxide, and get ready to release a mega-sized tower of chemistry!

MATERIALS NEEDED

Salon-strength hydrogen peroxide (6%)

Tall glass jar or vase

Food coloring

Spoon

Dish soap

Water

Small cup

1 package of active dry yeast

Large metal baking tray

Measuring cup

Rubber gloves

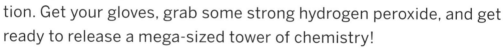

PROCEDURE

SAFETY NOTE: Hydrogen peroxide can irritate your skin when touched! Make sure you use your gloves when conducting this experiment! Never drink hydrogen peroxide!

1. Pour ½ cup of salon-strength hydrogen peroxide into your tall vase. (Salon-strength hydrogen peroxide will often show a 20-volume 6% percent solution. You can purchase this at a salon or beauty supply store.)

2. Add 10 drops of food coloring to the hydrogen peroxide in the vase, then stir to thoroughly color your peroxide.

3. Add 1-2 tablespoons of dish soap to the vase and swirl it around to combine the mixture.

4. Pour 4 tablespoons of warm water into your small cup. Add the packet of yeast and slowly stir the yeast into the water. Let it sit for a couple of minutes until it looks foamy and starts to give a bready smell.

5. Put the vase in the center of your baking tray. Then, dump the yeast into the vase and stand back!

6. After your foaming explosion is done, feel the sides of the vase. Is it warm? You've just created an exothermic (heat) reaction with your fizzing, oozing, dose of chemistry!

WHAT'S HAPPENING?

Hydrogen peroxide molecules consist of two hydrogen atoms and two oxygen atoms. When the peroxide is introduced to the yeast, the yeast acts as a catalyst to quickly break apart the oxygen from the hydrogen. This requires a lot of energy, which is released as heat, in what is called an exothermic reaction. All of the released oxygen bubbles quickly expand, combine with the foam made with the soap and water, and spill up and over the top of your vase!

IT'S A GAS!
The Magic of CO_2

Can you inflate a balloon without using your mouth? In grocery and party supply stores, workers use a container of compressed helium to fill balloons. Unless you buy your own helium tank, you'll need to rely on your mouth to pump air into balloons. With this experiment, you can save your breath and use the fizzing, bubbling power of chemistry to inflate a balloon with carbon dioxide gas.

MATERIALS NEEDED

20 oz water/soda bottle or flask

Baking soda

Balloon

Vinegar

Tablespoon

PROCEDURE

1. Place 2 tablespoons of baking soda into your bottle or flask. Take your balloon in hand and stretch it out a few times to increase the elasticity.

2. Secure the neck of the balloon around the top of your bottle and flip the bottle upside down to dump the baking soda into the balloon. Get as much of it in the balloon as possible, remove the balloon, and rinse out any baking soda that remains in the bottle. Set the balloon aside.

3. Fill your bottle halfway with vinegar. Then take your balloon and stretch the open end around the top of the bottle, making sure not to spill any baking soda inside the bottle.

4. Take your balloon and hold it up vertically above the mouth of the bottle. Stretch the balloon back and forth to dump the baking soda into the bottle.

5. Stand back and observe the reaction!

WHAT'S HAPPENING?

When baking soda and vinegar combine, they exchange parts of their atoms with each other, creating a fizzing, bubbling, reaction. This exchange of atomic particles completely changes the structure of the baking soda and vinegar, and forms a new compound called sodium acetate. What's left behind is a mixture of water and carbon dioxide gas. You can see the carbon dioxide gas as it expands and fills your balloon!

Grow a GIANT CARBON SNAKE

Chemistry experiments can cause amazing reactions like color-changing vials, exploding balls of fire, or gnarly formations growing out of beakers. Chemistry can also create some beautiful reactions, like those we see in the sky with a brilliant fireworks display! With this experiment, you'll explore the exciting side of chemistry by creating your very own dramatic display right on your driveway! By taking some common household ingredients, you'll grow a giant twisted carbon snake out of baking soda and powdered sugar!

SAFETY NOTE: Be careful! This experiment involves fuel, fire, and some serious chemistry! Be safe, and do this experiment with an adult!

MATERIALS NEEDED

Powdered sugar

Beaker or small glass with a flat rim

Baking soda

Spoon

Large Pyrex or heat-resistant bowl

91% rubbing alcohol

Wooden matches

Hose

128

PROCEDURE

SAFETY NOTE: This experiment should be performed outside, with adult participation. You'll be working with fire to cause a chemical reaction, resulting in a thick black carbon snake! Make sure you follow safety protocols, keep a hose nearby, and wear safety goggles! Do not try this on a windy day.

1. Pour 4 tablespoons of powdered sugar into your beaker. Then, add 1 tablespoon of baking soda and use your spoon to stir until the solids are thoroughly combined.

2. Hold your large bowl upside down over your beaker. Press the top of the beaker firmly into the center of the bowl. Then flip the bowl upside down while holding the beaker in the center. Lift the beaker, leaving a small, concentrated pile of baking soda and powdered sugar in the center of the bowl.

3. Pour 3 tablespoons of rubbing alcohol into your beaker. Then bring the beaker, the bowl, and your wooden matches outside to a clear flat area, preferably near a hose. If no hose is available, bring a full pitcher of water with you as an added precaution!

ADULT PARTICIPATION IS REQUIRED FOR THE REST OF THIS EXPERIMENT!

4. Have an adult pour the alcohol in the beaker into the bowl in a circular motion, around the outside of the pile of baking soda and powdered sugar.

5. Stand back! Have an adult light the matches, and then toss them into the alcohol. Lighting this will be similar to igniting lighter fluid in a barbecue. The fire will be warm and high, so make sure to stand away from it as you view the results of the chemical reaction!

6. You will initially see small black bubbles form on the surface of the powdered sugar and baking soda. After about one minute, however, you will see these bubbles concentrate in the center of the pile, and soon you'll see a giant black carbon snake grow out of the flames!

7. The fire will continue to burn until the fuel and baking soda and sugar mixture have been exhausted. If the flame has subsided, and you would like to end the demonstration, you can use your hose to slowly fill your bowl with water to suffocate the flames. Do not touch the bowl until it has cooled to a safe temperature!

*NEVER ADD FUEL TO YOUR SNAKE AFTER YOU'VE LIT THE ALCOHOL!
This can ignite your fuel source and cause a dangerous explosion!

WHAT'S HAPPENING?

Baking soda and sugar have a lot of carbon locked within their atomic structures. When they are heated up with a fuel source, it breaks down into sodium carbonate ash, water vapor, and carbon dioxide gas. The carbon dioxide gas pushes upwards through the ash, which causes it to grow from the flames.

RUMBLE

CHAPTER 10

RUMBLE

ERUPTING EARTH SCIENCE

SHAKE

Build an UNDERWATER VOLCANO

The vast expanses of the Earth's oceans are speckled with small rocky islands. How do these form in the middle of all of that water? Where does the rock come from? With this experiment, you'll explore the science of geology as you create the conditions of an underwater volcano. With just a little bit of time and some household materials, you'll erupt your way through geology as you create new lands with a volcano in a cup.

MATERIALS NEEDED

Small orange candle

Lighter or matches

Pyrex or heat-resistant measuring cup

Play sand

Water

Alum

Hot plate or pan half filled with water

Safety goggles

PROCEDURE

1. Light your candle and melt a thick layer of wax to pour into the Pyrex measuring cup. Tilt the candle slightly to allow the wax to drip down into the cup. Slowly rotate the candle to melt it evenly, and take care not to burn your fingers!

2. After you've melted a thick layer of wax, allow it to cool and resolidify. Then, pour a 1" layer of sand over the wax.

3. Fill the rest of your cup with water. If the water is murky, sprinkle some alum into the top layer of water and swirl it around with your fingers. After 10 minutes, it should be clear! (To learn how this works, refer to Build a Water Filter with Sand and Rocks on page 30.)

4. If you're using a hot plate, place the cup on the burner and turn it to its lowest setting.

   If you're using a pan, fill it halfway with water, and place the cup in the center. Turn the burner on to its lowest setting.

5. Let the cup warm up slowly. After approximately 5 minutes, turn the setting on the hot plate or on your stove to warm. Leave it on this setting so the cup can come to temperature slowly and evenly.

   (Warning: If you turn up the heat too quickly, even heat-resistant cups may shatter! Allow at least 5 minutes on the lowest setting before increasing the temperature, and wear your safety goggles just in case!)

6. Observe the layer of wax as your cup is warming up. Can you see your solid wax turning into liquid magma? You may begin to see air bubbles forming as the liquid allows trapped gases to escape.

7. After approximately 10 minutes, you should notice some volcanic activity under your ocean floor. Trapped gases may escape, and after a while, your pressurized magma will too!

8. When the lava has finished rising to the surface, turn the heat off your stove or hot plate, and allow your cup to completely cool before removing it. You can save your wax and reuse it for this experiment any time! Discard the rest as you would any other solid waste. Do not pour this down the drain!

WHAT'S HAPPENING?

In this experiment, the wax represents the mantle under the Earth's crust. At first, it is solid, compressed "rock," but when you apply heat underneath the mantle, it begins to melt, turning into magma! This heat creates a lot of pressure as trapped gases begin to carve through the rocks underwater. Once the pressure becomes too great, the magma bursts forth through the rocks and into the water above it, cooling and forming new land on the surface.

Jell-O EARTHQUAKE Engineering

Engineers have a lot to consider when they design, plan, and erect the buildings in a city. They need to consider wind, weather, the effects of the sun, the effects of gravity pulling down on a building, and of course, the chance of an earthquake shaking the ground beneath it! With this experiment, think like an engineer and use common household materials to design and build a toothpick tower that can withstand the rolling waves of an earthquake.

MATERIALS NEEDED

1 box of flavored gelatin

Glass baking dish

30 toothpicks

30 mini marshmallows

PROCEDURE

1. Make your Jell-O according to the instructions on the package. When you are finished, pour the liquid gelatin into the glass baking dish, and place it in your refrigerator to cool and set.

2. Now, it's time to think like an engineer! Plan the building that you'll construct with your toothpicks, and draw a few ideas out on paper before you begin.

3. Experiment with building different shapes with your toothpicks and marshmallows. Try constructing a square, then a triangle, then a cube. Which structure do you think will stand the longest during an earthquake?

4. Once you've created some basic structures, it's time to start building! Your toothpick tower should be at least two toothpick levels high. Try breaking toothpicks in half for a sturdier base.

5. When you've completed your toothpick tower, it's time to put it to the test! Set it aside, and retrieve your gelatin from the fridge. Bring your gelatin to a flat surface, and place the tower on top.

6. Now grab the sides of the baking dish, and start shaking! Will your building withstand the shaking of the ground below it? Are there any changes you can make to increase the stability of your building to increase its durability? If you change the height of the building or the width of the base, can you make it stronger?

WHAT'S HAPPENING?

You are thinking like an engineer when you design a building that can withstand a Jell-O earthquake! Engineers build models just like you did and test their structures to make sure they can survive extreme weather and natural disasters.

Sample the EARTH'S CORE

Do you know what lies underneath the ground at your feet? How do scientists know what makes up the Earth below the surface? Geologists study the rocks and minerals in the Earth's crust for a variety of reasons, including finding safe locations to build cities and developments, scouting for oil and mineral deposits, even to determine what the Earth looked like over its 4.5-billion year history! With this experiment, you'll work like a geologist and drill through the layers of the Earth, earning a sweet sampling of the Earth's core.

MATERIALS NEEDED

Box of white cake mix and ingredients to prepare it

6 bowls

Red, blue, green, yellow food coloring

Muffin tin

Cupcake liners

6 spoons

Toothpick

Butter knife

Clear drinking straw

30

20

10

PROCEDURE

1. Prepare the cake mix according the instructions on the package. Then, divide the batter into six bowls.

2. Use the food coloring to create the colors of the rainbow. Mix red and blue to create purple, red and yellow for orange, then red, green, blue, and yellow. Use 8-10 drops of food coloring in each bowl to create a saturated color.

3. Line your muffin pan with cupcake liners. For each cupcake, layer one spoonful of each color in the following order: purple, blue, green, red, orange, and yellow. Use the spoon to lightly smooth each layer on top of the other without mixing them together.

4. Bake the cupcakes as instructed on the box and remove them from the oven. Allow them to cool.

5. Remove the wrapper from a cupcake, and use your knife to cut the cupcake in half. You should see several layers present in your cupcakes! These layers represent the Earth's crust!

6. Now, get ready to drill like a geologist! Push a straw down through the center of a cupcake, twisting slowly as you "drill" down to the bottom. Give it a final twist, and then pull your straw straight up! What do you see?

7. Cut the end of the straw with your sample, isolating your sample into a small piece. Use the rest of your straw to sample the core of another cupcake! Trim the sample away and set it next to the first sample. Repeat this step two or three times, and compare your samples.

WHAT'S HAPPENING?

Geologists study the Earth by drilling small hollow tubes through layers of rocks, sand, minerals, and fossils that make up the Earth's crust. The samples they extract from the tubes give them useful information about history, climate change, and more.

COOKIE
Continents and
Ocean Erosion

Cookies and milk can make for a great afternoon snack, but they can also be used for science! With this experiment, you'll snack your way through the science of erosion, oceanic currents, and environmental science. With milky oceans and crumbly cookie continents, you'll have the power to make waters rise, create your own islands, and even melt polar ice caps!

MATERIALS NEEDED

GINGERBREAD COOKIE RECIPE

6 tablespoons unsalted butter, softened (not melted)

¾ cups packed dark brown sugar

½ cup molasses

1 egg

2 tsp vanilla extract

1 tsp grated lemon peel

3 cups all-purpose flour

3 tsp ground ginger

1 ½ tsp baking powder

1 ¼ tsp cinnamon

¾ tsp baking soda

¼ tsp salt

¼ tsp ground cloves

ADDITIONAL MATERIALS FOR CONTINENTAL COOKIE PLATES:

Large glass baking dish
(or large flat baking tray)

Milk

Blue food coloring

Ice tray

World map printout

Butter knife

Toothpick

Nonstick baking sheet

PROCEDURE

1. In a big bowl, whisk the butter and sugar together until it becomes fluffy. Beat in the molasses, egg, vanilla, and lemon peel. In a separate bowl, whisk together all the dry ingredients. Gradually beat the dry mix into the wet mix.

2. Divide the dough in half and shape into discs. Wrap it in plastic wrap and chill in the fridge for at least 30 minutes.

3. While you're waiting for the dough to chill, prepare your polar ice caps. Pour one cup of milk into a measuring cup, and add 10 drops of blue food coloring. Stir to combine until you reach a deep blue color. Then pour your milk into an ice tray and place it in the freezer.

4. Preheat your oven to 350 degrees. On a lightly floured surface, roll out your dough to approximately 1/4" thickness.

5. Print out a world map and cut out the continents. Place them over your cookie dough, and use a butter knife and a toothpick to trace your continent shapes and cut them out. Once you have your continent cookies, it's time to bake them!

6. Place them on a nonstick baking sheet, and bake for 7-9 minutes. Then cool for at least 15 minutes before continuing with the experiment.

7. Once the cookies have cooled, place them in your baking dish according to their placement in the world. You can refer to the world map you used for proper continent placement.

8. Pour a small amount of milk into the baking dish, just enough to form a milky ocean around your cookie continents, but not enough to completely submerge them.

9. Finally, add your polar ice caps to the North and South Poles. Now it's time to sit back and observe what happens as the ice caps melt, and your oceans rise! Place your baking dish in a warm area, and monitor your cookie continents over the course of 30 minutes.

WHAT'S HAPPENING?

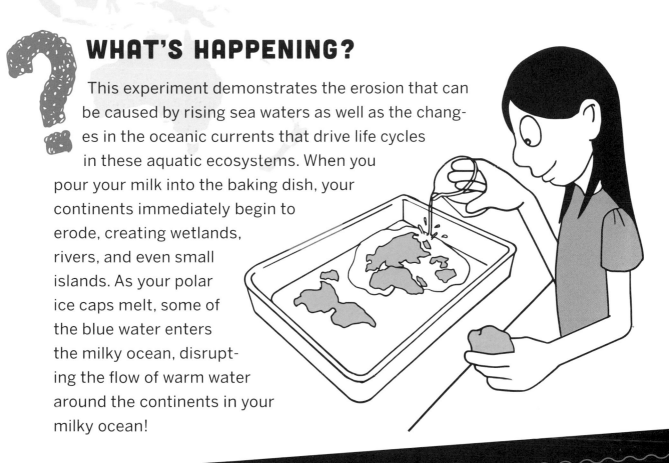

This experiment demonstrates the erosion that can be caused by rising sea waters as well as the changes in the oceanic currents that drive life cycles in these aquatic ecosystems. When you pour your milk into the baking dish, your continents immediately begin to erode, creating wetlands, rivers, and even small islands. As your polar ice caps melt, some of the blue water enters the milky ocean, disrupting the flow of warm water around the continents in your milky ocean!

TAKE IT FURTHER

Can you change the impacts of rising waters on continental lands? Think like an engineer and build barriers in vulnerable coastal regions to see if you can block the rising waters from eroding away the coastlines

PLAY-DOH
Plate Tectonics

Did you know that the Earth under your feet is constantly in motion? You may not be able to feel it, but the continents, the ocean floor, and the Earth's crust itself are constantly moving around, sliding on a molten surface of liquid magma. With this experiment, you'll explore the science of plate tectonics while moving continents, making mountains, and breaking land apart with massive shifts. Grab some clay, and get ready to set these forces into motion with Play-Doh plate tectonics!

MATERIALS NEEDED

Wax paper

Rolling pin

3 different colors of Play-Doh

Butter knife

Large glass baking dish

Vegetable oil

Tape

PROCEDURE

1. Tape a long piece of wax paper onto a flat surface. Choose three colors of Play-Doh.

2. Roll each piece of dough until it is about ¼" thick. Then layer three different colors on top of each other, with colors going from dark on the bottom to light on top. Don't press the layers into each other, as you'll want them to move about easily!

    The bottom layer of your Play-Doh will represent the mantle of the Earth. The second layer will represent oceanic crust, while the top layer will represent continental crust.

3. Trim the outer edges of the Play-Doh with your butter knife so that all the colors are visible and the edges are even. Roll the extra trimmings into a ball and set it aside. Cut the layered slab in half.

4. Pour 3 tablespoons of vegetable oil into your baking dish and use your hand to smear it around, evenly coating the dish. Take your 2 triple-layered dough pieces, and use your hand to lubricate the bottom of each one. Then place both layered dough pieces into the baking dish.

5. Now, it's time to crash your tectonic plates into each other! Put your hands on both pieces of Play-Doh and slowly slide them together, so that one piece is being pushed underneath the second piece. This is called a convergent boundary, and can cause mountains to form.

6. Pull your Play-Doh pieces apart and smooth them out. This time, press the sides of them together, and pull the upper layer (the continental plate) away, while pushing the lower layers upwards. This represents a divergent boundary, where layers of crust pull away from each other, and magma comes up from below, creating new layers of Earth crust!

7. Pull your Play-Doh pieces apart and smooth them out. Place them right next to each other, so each side is touching the other. Then take your ball of dough and roll it into a snake shape. Lay the snake over both pieces of dough, creating a river that spans both continental plates.

8. Now, you're going to cause an earthquake! Press your two pieces of dough into each other, and then suddenly shift directions, pushing one piece of dough up and the other down. This is called a transform boundary and it can transform land on the surface of the Earth!

WHAT'S HAPPENING?

The surface of the Earth is broken up into several large tectonic plates that move around on a layer of molten magma deep within the Earth. When they meet, they can create the boundaries you modeled with your Play-Doh. Convergent boundaries form as tectonic plates push into each other, and one falls below the other, sinking into the mantle. The other plate rises above, creating a new mountain range. Divergent boundaries occur when plates pull apart and magma from the mantle is pushed to the surface. This cools and hardens into a new layer of crust. Transform boundaries occur as plates press into each other and shift apart with great pressure, causing huge earthquakes and dramatic transformations of the land!

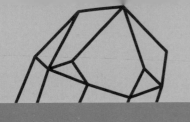

SHIMMER

CHAPTER 11

SQUISH

GEOLOGY AT ITS BEST

STACK

Molten Magma
ROCK CANDY

Igneous rocks are made from lava and magma, formed deep within the Earth's crust. When magma is pushed up to the surface of the earth, it forms a volcano, from which the magma escapes, turning into red-hot liquid lava! This lava spews out of the volcano, blasting out of its top, and can sometimes pour down the sides, resulting in rivers of oozing red hot rock. Once it cools, it can form a glassy rock, or a porous pumice stone. With this experiment, you'll create your own red-hot molten magma candy, by creating an environment of intense heat to melt down sugar rocks, and create your own edible igneous rocks!

MATERIALS NEEDED

½ cup of light corn syrup

1 cup of sugar

1 tsp of water

Pyrex or heat-resistant 2-cup measuring cup

Aluminum foil

Food coloring

Oven mitts

Metal spoons

Microwave

Cup of cold water

PROCEDURE

SAFETY NOTE: This project requires adult participation. The molten sugar magma is hot enough to cause serious burns if it spills onto your skin.

1. Mix the corn syrup, sugar, and water into your mixing cup. Use your spoon to fold everything over until thoroughly mixed.

2. Cover a flat surface with aluminum foil. You'll want a space that is at least 2' x 2', to give you enough coverage when you start working with your magma.

3. Open your food coloring and set the bottles in the corner of your foil, with a spoon next to them. This way, you'll have everything ready once you bring your magma to your candy station.

4. Bring your oven mitts, a spoon, and your measuring cup over to your microwave. Microwave the sugar mixture on high power for 3-7 minutes, or until the mixture is bubbling to the surface and just beginning to turn to a golden color.

5. While your mixture is microwaving, pour cold water into a cup. When you think your mixture is ready, take a spoonful and drip it into the cup. If the mixture forms a blob or puddle at the bottom of the cup, it's not ready yet. If it makes a cracking sound and seems to freeze into shape, you're ready!

6. Have an adult bring the measuring cup of magma to your rock station.

SAFETY NOTE: When this "liquid magma" comes out of the microwave, it will be VERY HOT. If it spills on you it will cause burns! The transport of magma from microwave to work area should only be done by an adult wearing oven mitts on both hands.

7. Now, it's time to get creative! Drizzle spoonfuls of molten magma onto your work surface. You can add some drops of food coloring and use your spoon to swirl them into your molten lava! What kinds of patterns can you make? Can you sculpt rivers of lava flow? Can you create glass sculptures with your lava?

8. Drop a small puddle of magma onto the work surface. Once it cools, pick it up and try to bend it into a ball, or twirl it into a spiral shape.

9. Let your molten magma candy cool completely before removing it from the foil. Pick off any remaining pieces of foil that remain attached. Now, it's ready to eat!

CLEANING TIP! Your measuring cup will be a sticky glassy mess when this is done! To clean your cup, simply soak it in hot sudsy water. After a short while, all the sugar will be dissolved by the water.

WHAT'S HAPPENING?

When you melt down the sugar crystals, you are replicating the same conditions that melt rocks deep in the Earth. All rocks are made with crystal-like structures of atoms, that link together and build up to form the rocks we see around us. When these rocks are put under intense heat deep inside the Earth, they can melt down to form magma. When this erupts to the surface as lava, that lava cools and crystallizes to form new igneous rocks.

SALT CRYSTAL TOWER

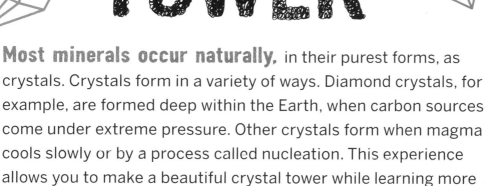

Most minerals occur naturally, in their purest forms, as crystals. Crystals form in a variety of ways. Diamond crystals, for example, are formed deep within the Earth, when carbon sources come under extreme pressure. Other crystals form when magma cools slowly or by a process called nucleation. This experience allows you to make a beautiful crystal tower while learning more about nucleation.

MATERIALS NEEDED

Safety goggles

Toilet paper tube

3 tablespoons household ammonia

3 tablespoons laundry bluing

Paper plate

1 tablespoon table salt

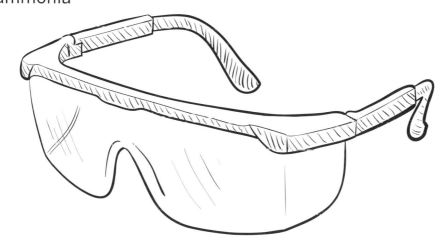

PROCEDURE

1. Put on your safety goggles!

2. Clean your toilet paper tube of any remaining bits of paper.

3. Using your tablespoon, measure and pour the ammonia and bluing on to the paper plate. Make sure you are in a well-ventilated area or next to an open window. Ammonia is incredibly potent with its burning odor.

4. Add the salt and gently stir the solution.

5. Place your toilet paper tube in the center of your plate and let it sit. After about 30 minutes, you'll begin to see a reaction. After 12-24 hours, you'll have a full-grown crystal tower!

WHAT'S HAPPENING?

Nucleation begins when a mineral-rich, liquid solution (like your salt mixture) evaporates. As the water evaporates, the atoms of the minerals slowly come together. Once there is a large group of them, they will begin to attract more atoms of that mineral at a faster rate. These atoms link together in regular patterns, forming crystals.

Metamorphic CANDY BARS:
The Science of the Squish

Metamorphic rocks are igneous or sedimentary rocks that are subjected to extreme heat and pressure deep within the Earth's crust. These pressures can force one type of rock into another type of rock, creating a whole new color and shape! They often leave warped swirls of colors on the surface of the rocks. In this demonstration, you'll force your own heat and pressure on a candy bar rock to discover the processes behind their formations, and make your own metamorphic rock that you can eat!

MATERIALS NEEDED

Snickers bar
(or candy containing nuts, caramel, nougat, and chocolate)

Aluminum foil

Large pan

Square baking dish

Stove

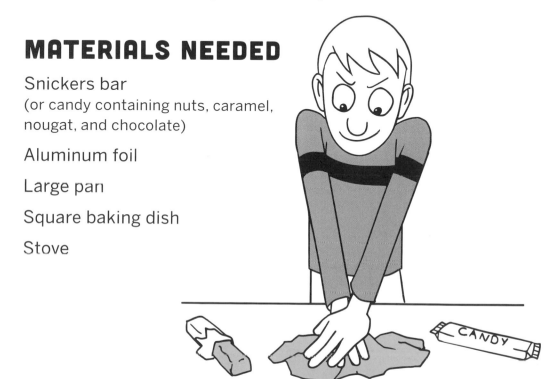

30

20

10

PROCEDURE

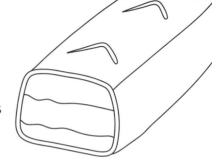

1. Break your candy bar in half and examine the layers of your sedimentary rock. Set one half of your rock aside for later.

2. Wrap one of the rock halves in aluminum foil. Put your pan on top and press down hard! This will mimic the pressures found deep within the Earth.

3. Open your foil and examine your newly pressed rock. How have the layers changed? Are there any rocks you've seen in nature that remind you of this?

4. Put your pan on the stove and turn it to med/high heat. Rewrap your candy bar in the foil and add it to the pan. Take your baking dish and press down on your wrapped candy, for 7-10 seconds.

5. Remove the foil from the pan and open it. What happened? As your rock cools, observe how it has changed through heat and pressure.

6. Examine the colors and layers of the sedimentary rock in the half you set aside earlier. After examining the layers and comparing them to the differences in your new metamorphic rock, it's time to chow down!

WHAT'S HAPPENING?

Metamorphic rocks form when igneous or sedimentary rocks are melted and crushed within the Earth's mantle. The intense heat and pressure can partially melt and compress the rocks, turning them into completely different rocks. When you heat your candy bar on the stove, and press it with your baking dish, you can see that the components of your rocks shift around. This forms new patterns and forces some of the outer chocolate layers into the inside of your rock, creating a new metamorphic rock.

Seven-Layer Sedimentary Crackers

Sedimentary rocks have been around for billions of years, and can be found in formations like sandstone and limestone. Sedimentary rocks can be found anywhere dirt, rocks, and sand can collect and layer on top of each other. They're found in deserts, riverbeds, and great canyons and valleys. With this demonstration, you will create your own sedimentary rocks with seven-layer sediment bars that you can eat!

MATERIALS NEEDED

1½ cups of graham cracker crumbs

Gallon-sized freezer bag

Rolling pin

½ cup of butter

13 x 9 glass baking dish

Mixing spoon

½ cup semisweet chocolate chips

½ cup butterscotch chips

1 cup flaked coconut

1 cup chopped walnuts or pecans

1 can (14 oz) sweetened condensed milk

PROCEDURE

1. Preheat your oven to 350 degrees. While your oven is preheating, start preparing your graham cracker crumbs. Place 9 graham crackers in your freezer bag and seal it so it is airtight. Use your rolling pin to smash the graham crackers until the texture resembles sand.

2. Melt 1 stick of butter until you have ½ cup of melted butter. Pour this evenly into the baking dish. Then sprinkle even layers of graham cracker crumbs into the butter. Use your spoon to thoroughly mix the graham cracker crumbs and butter until the crumbs are evenly coated. Then use your spoon to press the crumbs into the bottom of the dish, forming an even, solid layer of sandy crumbs.

3. Layer the rest of your ingredients in the following order: butterscotch chips, chocolate chips, coconut flakes, and chopped nuts. Make sure each ingredient is layered evenly before moving on to the next layer.

4. Open the can of sweetened condensed milk and drizzle it in a crisscross pattern over the top of your ingredients, forming a smooth, even layer over the top.

5. Place the baking dish in the oven, and cook your sedimentary cookies for approximately 25-30 minutes, or until the top is lightly browned.

6. Let the cookies cool for 15 minutes, then move them to your freezer for an additional 15 minutes to continue cooling and setting.

WHAT'S HAPPENING?

In this activity, you are replicating the formation of sedimentary rocks by forming your own layers of sediment! Your graham cracker crust represents a silty layer of sand and rock. The butterscotch and chocolate chips are remains of living things from long ago, with larger pecan rocks and coconut plant matter layering over the top of it. The final layer of condensed milk acts as another layer of sediment and water, compressing everything down and solidifying them in place.

Grow Your Own CRYSTAL GARDEN

Have you ever seen a rock with angular, sparkly objects on it? These objects are called crystals, and they can form in a variety of ways. Some of them are formed by intense heat and pressure beneath the Earth's crust. Others are formed when magma cools at a very slow and steady rate, allowing for structured crystal growth. Still others are formed when minerals dissolved in water evaporate, leaving a budding growth of crystals that are dazzling to see. With this experiment, you'll be making your own dissolved mineral crystals, and grow a colorful rock garden at the same time!

MATERIALS NEEDED

Hammer

Large piece of charcoal

Scissors

Unused kitchen sponge

Household ammonia

Laundry bluing

Salt

Distilled water

Small pie tin

Spoon

Safety goggles

Food coloring (optional)

PROCEDURE

A NOTE ON SAFETY: Take this experiment outside or to a well-ventilated area. The ammonia has a very pungent odor and is not safe to breathe in close quarters!

1. Before you begin, clean your pie tin of any stickers, plastic, or adhesive.

2. Use your hammer to break your charcoal into several small pieces. Use your scissors to cut your sponge into small squares.

3. Pour 1 tablespoon each of ammonia, laundry bluing (this can be found in the laundry aisle of any grocery store), distilled water, and salt into the pie tin. Use your spoon to stir the ingredients until they are thoroughly combined.

4. Place your charcoal and sponges into the pie pan, putting them at least ½" apart.

5. To add a splash of color to your garden, place one or two drops off food coloring onto each surface.

6. Wait approximately 30 minutes, and then check the progress of your crystal garden. Periodically check the progress of your crystals throughout the day. After approximately 24 hours, you should have some significant crystal growth!

WHAT'S HAPPENING?

You are growing crystals from evaporated salt! A chemical reaction between the ammonia and bluing breaks down iron and sodium, increasing the salt content for faster crystal growth. The crystals form in a process called nucleation, when a cluster of atoms begins to group together in a crystal formation. Once the first crystal forms, others quickly build onto it, resulting in the beautiful structures you see in your crystal garden!

CRYSTAL
Snowflake Ornaments

Snow has long captured the imagination and delighted children. Who can resist its delicate, white, flakes—each with its own unique pattern? Snowflakes are crystals, just like the crystal rocks you find on the ground. With this experiment, you'll mimic the process of snowflake growth and bring to life the magic of snow, while making your very own mineral snowflakes!

MATERIALS NEEDED

¼ cup of hot tap water

Almost boiling water

Tall wide-mouthed jar

2 pipe cleaners

Scissors

Pencil

Borax laundry powder

Spoon

Safety goggles

30

20

10

PROCEDURE

1. Heat a kettle or pot of water until it is almost boiling. While waiting for the water to boil, add ¼ cup of hot tap water to your jar. This will allow the jar to come to a higher temperature without shattering

2. Lay your pipe cleaners out in front of you. Take one of the pipe cleaners and cut it into thirds. Fold these small pieces around the end of the other pipe cleaner so that you form a 6-pronged snowflake.

3. Take the free end of your long pipe cleaner, and wind it around your pencil. Hold it up against the outside of the jar to make sure that the snowflake will be able to fit inside of it without touching its sides or bottom. Wind the pipe cleaner over the pencil to reduce the length, and trim the points of your snowflakes as needed.

4. When the water is almost to a boil, turn the heat down and slowly add water to the jar, one splash at time, until it's half full.

5. Add 3 tablespoons of Borax to the water, stirring to dissolve. Then add 1 tablespoon at a time, while stirring, until you can no longer dissolve any more Borax in the solution and you see particles collecting at the bottom of the jar.

6. Lower your pipe cleaner snowflake into the jar, with the pencil lying over the mouth. After 60 minutes, check the jar. It should take about 12-24 hours for the crystals to fully form on your snowflake.

7. After 60 minutes, check the jar. It should take about 12-24 hours for the crystals to form on your snowflake.

WHAT'S HAPPENING?

When you add the Borax to hot water, you get a supersaturated solution. The hot water allows more solids to be dissolved into it, as atoms move around at a rapid pace. As the water cools, these particles group back together and some of them latch onto the pipe cleaner, forming long crystal structures. Snowflakes are formed in a similar process, as water vapor freezes onto small dust particles in clouds and forms into small crystals that fall to the ground as snow.

HAIR-RAISING Jell-O Stalagmites

Stalagmites are tall pillars of minerals formed by dripping water and mineral deposits. They can often be found growing up from cave floors. If you don't have any caves nearby, don't despair! You can create stalagmites in your kitchen and examine them up close—just like a cave explorer. With this experiment, you'll combine Jell-O, a balloon, and a full head of hair to build some fantastic geology with the power of static electricity.

MATERIALS NEEDED

Balloon

Unflavored gelatin

Wool, fleece, or your full head of hair

Plate

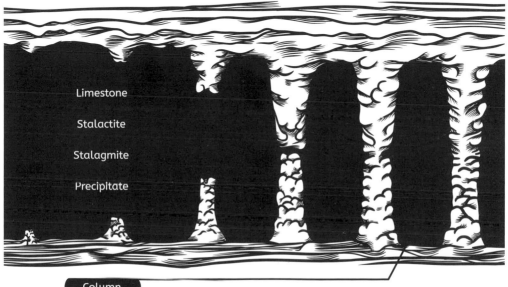

Limestone

Stalactite

Stalagmite

Precipitate

Column

30

20

10

PROCEDURE

1. Inflate your balloon until it is large and firm, and set it aside.

2. Open your packet of unflavored gelatin and empty it onto a flat surface.

3. Charge your balloon with static electricity by rubbing it on your fabric, or your full head of hair! You will know when it's ready by the way the hair or fabric sticks to your balloon!

4. Gently place your charged balloon over the gelatin. You will need to get really close, and you may need to lightly touch it. Once the gelatin clings to the balloon, slowly pull away to get your stalagmites!

WHAT'S HAPPENING?

As you rub your balloon on your head or sweater, it knocks a bunch of electrons off the surface, and onto your balloon, giving your balloon a negative charge. These electrons seek out protons to balance the charges into an equilibrium. When you bring the balloon to the Jell-O, these particles are attracted to each other and stick together! As they reach up to the balloon, the particles of charged gelatin build towering formations that look like the stalagmites found in caves!

TAKE IT FURTHER

In caverns, stalactite structures grow down from the ceiling, while stalagmites build up from the ground. Their appearance is similar to the structures created with the gelatin and the balloon. Try this experiment with flavored and unflavored gelatin to see if you get the same results. You can also try this experiment with a variety of dry spices to see which ones will yield the most static cling, and thus the tallest towers of static stalagmites!

PUSH

CHAPTER 12

PULL

ALL CHARGED UP ABOUT MAGNETS

SWING

30

20

10

DANCING
Magnetic Slime

There's really nothing better than a good, old-fashioned batch of gooey slime. With the sticky, putty-like material, you can stretch it, slap it, or even print patterns onto it. With this experiment, you'll give slime a new twist, and make a slime that can even dance. All you'll need are some iron filings and some magnets, and you'll enjoy a front row seat to the laws of magnetic attraction.

MATERIALS NEEDED

Small cup

Water

Borax

2 spoons

Mixing bowl

8 oz bottle of white craft glue

Food coloring

Iron fillings

Plate

Magnets

Plastic sandwich or storage bag

PROCEDURE

1. Fill a small cup halfway with warm water. Add 2 teaspoons of Borax and stir until thoroughly combined, then set the cup aside.

2. Dump all of your glue into the mixing bowl. Fill the empty glue bottle with water and swirl it around to remove the excess glue. Pour the water into the bowl, and stir the glue and water mixture to thoroughly combine.

3. Add a few drops of food coloring and stir to combine. Then add a generous amount (approximately 2 tablespoons) of iron filings into the glue and water mixture. Then, stir to thoroughly combine.

4. Add 2 tablespoons of the Borax water mixture into the mixing bowl, and stir to combine. You'll immediately notice it start to clump together into a solid slime mixture!

5. Remove the solid mass of slime mixture and set it onto your plate. Use your hands to play with it until it reaches a putty consistency.

6. Congratulations, you've just made metallic slime! Now, you can place your magnet near your slime to make it dance. Any time you place a magnet near it, it will react to it, and move to meet the magnet.

7. When you are finished playing with your slime, you can place it in your storage bag to store for future use.

WHAT'S HAPPENING?

The glue-and-water mixture contains millions of strong and flexible molecule chains called polymers. When you add the Borax, it immediately binds to those chains, linking them all together. When you add the iron filings, the polymers wrap around them, holding them back from jumping to the magnet. Instead, they reach out through the slime, causing the dancing, twisting, and twirling you see when you bring your magnet near.

Magnetic Cereal: Where's the Iron?

Are you getting a healthy dose of vitamins and minerals in your daily diet? We often look for foods that are fortified with vitamins and minerals like iron and calcium, because we know that they are important to our bodies and how they function. However, we may not realize exactly what these minerals look like. With this experiment, you'll separate iron from cereal and isolate it with a magnet, while holding this vital mineral right in your hands!

MATERIALS NEEDED

Wheat flake cereal
(fortified with iron)

Plate

1-quart freezer bag

1 cup of water

Magnets

PROCEDURE

1. Take a few flakes of the cereal and put them on your plate. Use your fingers to break them up into smaller pieces and place your magnet near them. Do you see any flakes sticking? They stick to your magnet because they have iron in them!

2. Now, fill your freezer bag with one cup of cereal. Use your hands to crunch the flakes until they have all broken down into tiny pieces.

3. Next, fill the bag halfway with warm water. Tightly seal the bag, leaving some air inside, then vigorously shake the bag to thoroughly mix the water and cereal. This will allow the cereal to dissolve and break apart in the water.

4. Once the mixture has turned into a brown soup, set it on a flat surface and let it sit for approximately 20 minutes.

5. After the cereal has had some time to dissolve and rest, carefully pick the bag up and grab your magnet. It's time to start looking for iron! Take your magnet and drag it around on the outside of the bag, near the bottom. Swirl the magnet around in a circular motion, and keeping the magnet on the bag, drag it up above the water line.

   Do you see iron stuck to your magnet? This is the iron that's inside your cereal!

WHAT'S HAPPENING?

Any food item that is fortified with iron actually has food-grade metallic iron inside it. This iron is embedded deep within the cereal flakes, but when you break the flakes down, you can see some of the pieces. Because iron is magnetic, you are able to attract isolated pieces to your magnets. Iron is important for our bodies to function; it is present in our blood cells as hemoglobin, the compound that carries oxygen to the tissues in our bodies.

The Magnet-Powered PENDULUM

Pendulums have been around for thousands of years, and have a lot of uses. They have helped people keep track of time, for example, and measure seismic waves during an earthquake. A pendulum works with the force of gravity, pulling an object down with a constant motion, and then swinging back to its original position again. With this experiment, you'll add an additional force to your pendulum: the force of magnetism. With just a few magnets, you can completely alter the direction of your pendulum, all while exploring the concept of magnetic fields and how they affect the objects around them.

MATERIALS NEEDED

Chair or stool

3 strong magnets

Galvanized (zinc-plated) nut

Ruler

18" piece of string

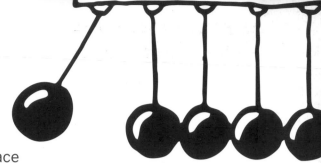

PROCEDURE

1. Place your chair on a flat surface. Place your magnets directly under the bar that connects the legs of your chair. If your magnets are marked with a north or south pole, test which end is attracted to your nut. Make sure to place that end upwards.

2. Using your ruler to measure the distance, place your three magnets in a triangular shape, 6" apart from each other.

3. Take the plated nut and tie it to a string, then tie the other end to the underside of the chair above your magnets. Adjust the length of the string so that the nut hangs about 1" above the magnets.

4. Once your magnets are in place, it's time to swing your pendulum! Bring the nut towards your body, so that it just passes the closest magnet. Then slowly let it go, so that it falls in a straight line away from you.

5. Observe the nut as it swings in motion. Can you tell when the nut becomes caught in the magnetic fields of your magnets?

6. Try swinging your pendulum again, only this time, swing it in a circular motion towards the magnets. Observe the changes in the patterns of the swing as it gets caught in the magnetic field.

WHAT'S HAPPENING?

When you swing a pendulum without magnets, gravity will pull it down, and it will continue swinging on a consistent path until it loses energy and it comes to a stop. When you add magnets around your pendulum and catch the galvanized nut in their magnetic fields, you can change the way in which the pendulum swings.

Recording
MAGNETIC
Fields

There are many invisible forces at work within our planet. Gravity is a force that pulls us down toward the core of the planet. Air pressure presses down with the weight of the atmosphere. Magnetism is a force that surrounds our planet and stretches out into space, deflecting solar wind energy that would otherwise break apart our atmosphere. We may not always be able to see these forces, but we can measure their effects through the explorations of science. With this experiment, you'll be able to visualize the magnetic field of common magnets, and gain some understanding as to how they work.

MATERIALS NEEDED

Ceramic bar magnet

Neodymium magnet

Refrigerator magnet

Iron filings

Glass from a picture frame

Pencil and paper

PROCEDURE

1. Place a ceramic bar magnet on a flat surface. If you're using glass from a picture frame, carefully remove it from the frame and then lay it over your magnet, balanced so it lies flat.

2. Take a pinch of iron filings, and slowly sprinkle them directly onto the glass over and around your magnet. Make sure to sprinkle even amounts as you circle your magnet.

3. Lightly tap the glass to allow the rest of the filings to fall into place along the magnetic fields.

4. Sketch what you see on a piece of paper, and label the magnet that you used.

5. Carefully lift your glass and remove the magnet from underneath. Use a piece of paper to scrape your iron filings back into their container.

6. Repeat the steps with your neodymium and refrigerator magnets. If you have any other magnets in your home, do the same with these! Draw your results on your piece of paper, and label which magnets you used and what their magnetic fields look like.

WHAT'S HAPPENING?

The Earth is surrounded by an invisible force called the magnetic field that stretches far out from the North and South poles. Materials like iron, steel, and cobalt interact with this magnetic field due to the alignment of particles within their atoms. When you scatter iron filings over a magnet, you're able to see the lines of this magnetic field, just as they would appear if we could see them around the Earth!

Make Your Own Bottle-Cork COMPASS

People have long used compasses to navigate everything from vast expanses of oceans to trails that snake through forests and mountains. Compasses are aligned with the invisible magnetic fields that surrounds the Earth. With this experiment, you'll follow in the footsteps of history's greatest navigators and make your very own working compass, right at home, with just a few household materials!

MATERIALS NEEDED

Sewing needle

Magnet

Wine cork

Bowl of water

Scissors

PROCEDURE

NOTE: This experiment works best with a strong magnet, such as a rare earth neodymium magnet. Refrigerator magnets will work, too, although you may need to rub your needle with it several times in order to magnetize it.

1. Magnetize your sewing needle by rubbing the magnet against it in the same direction 12 times. Once your needle is magnetized, set it aside.

2. Take your scissors and cut the end off of the cork. Make sure that both ends remain flat! You should end up with a cork disk that is approximately ¼" tall.

3. Push the sewing needle through the side of the cork so that it makes a horizontal line. You may need to use the flat end of your scissors to help push the needle through.

4. Float your compass in the bowl of water! As the cork compass spins, pay attention to the direction where the needle is pointing. Is it pointing north?

5. Spin the compass around, or place it so that it is pointing to the east or west. Will it spin to face north?

WHAT'S HAPPENING?

Sewing needles themselves are not magnetic, as the electrons within their atoms are not lined up in accordance to the Earth's magnetic field. However, when you run your magnet along the length of the sewing needle several times, you force these particles to line up evenly in the same direction. This magnetizes the needle, while the cork and water remove the resistance of forces like gravity and friction. The cork can spin freely and aligns with the magnetic field!

WHOOSH

CHAPTER 13

SWISH

THE SCIENCE OF WEATHER

FLUTTER

SNOW in SUMMER

Experimenting with chemistry can bring forth a lot of fun experiences, but did you know it can also lead to snow? You don't even have to wait for the winter months to arrive before you can play with the fluffy white stuff. By exploring the science of super-absorbing polymers, you can create a fake snow storm in your kitchen all year long! Find out which liquids create the best snow as you create a winter wonderland of science.

MATERIALS NEEDED

3 clear glasses

Water

Orange juice

Tomato juice

3 small bowls

Sodium polyacrylate powder*

*You can purchase this "fake snow powder" online, or you can purchase the powder from a gardening supply store (look for gardening water crystals) or obtain it from disposable diapers! If using diapers, cut open the ends of the diapers, and peel apart the layers. Place the middle cotton layer in a plastic baggie, close the baggie, and shake it around. Pour the collected powder crystals into a bowl for the experiment.

30

20

10

PROCEDURE

1. Fill one glass with ½ cup water, the other with ½ cup orange juice, and the last with ½ cup of tomato juice.

2. In each of the small bowls, pour ½ teaspoon of "fake snow powder" into little mounds. Use your finger to indent a small crater in the center of each mound.

3. Pour a small amount of water into the center of the powder in one of the bowls. Pour the orange juice in the powder of another bowl, and tomato juice into the powder of the last bowl. Keep pouring until the powder has absorbed as much liquid as possible.

4. Now, pour ½ tsp of your "fake snow powder" into each glass. Does each liquid absorb the polymer at the same rate? Tilt your glasses to the side, or even try turning them upside down!

5. Now, it's time to build a snowstorm in your kitchen! Place 1 tsp of "fake snow powder" in your hands. Pour a generous splash of water in your hands, and within a couple of seconds you should have an eruption of snow powder billowing out of your hands!

6. If you have a lot of fake snow powder, pour ¼ cup into a small glass. Then fill it with water, and watch as you create a fountain of erupting fluffy snow!

7. Experiment with different amounts of water and powder to create the perfect snowstorm! Then try to push your powder into a snowball! Can you build a snowman with it?

WHAT'S HAPPENING?

Absorbent polymers absorb 200-300 times their mass in water, and release it slowly over a long period of time. You can add just about any water-based liquid to this substance and watch it puff up into a fluffy consistency! Once you're finished playing with it, leave it out to evaporate. The crystals will shrink down to the tiny powder particles with which you started.

Build a
TORNADO
CHAMBER

Tornadoes are some of the most dramatic and destructive forces in nature. With wind speeds that can reach over 300 mph, they can rip through the landscape, uprooting trees, blasting through buildings, and leaving a path of destruction that can span several miles over the countryside. With this experiment, you'll learn how tornadoes can form, and build a tornado chamber and your very own swirling fog tornado!

MATERIALS NEEDED

Large cardboard box
(at least 24" tall)

Box cutter

Ruler

Duct tape

Scissors

Small electric fan

Black paint
and paintbrush

Medium-sized bowl

Dry ice

Hammer

Tongs

Insulated
safety gloves

Plastic
cling wrap

PROCEDURE

SAFETY NOTE: This experiment requires adult participation with the extensive use of a box cutter.

1. Stand your box up so that it is taller than it is wide. To make the tornado chamber, you will need to cut a ½" wide, 20" long (or as long as the box allows) vertical slit on the far left of all four side panels of your box. The slit should be at least 1" away from the left edge, and should run almost the length of each side.

2. On the front panel of your box, cut a large window starting 1" to the right of your vertical slit and ending about 1" from the right edge of the front of the box.

3. Cut open a large hole on the bottom of the box, large enough that you can fit it over your bowl with ease.

4. Finally, sit your small desktop fan on top of your box, in the center. Cut out a hole that is slightly smaller than your fan, so your fan can sit on top of the box, resting over the hole.

5. Paint the inside of the box black and allow it to fully dry before moving on to the creation of your tornado.

6. Tape the sides of your box shut, and make sure to duct tape over any edges or openings that haven't been cut out.

7. Cut a piece of plastic cling wrap so that it will fit over the entire window, as well as some extra over the sides. Stretch the cling wrap so that it will fit tightly over the window, creating a clear viewing surface. Then use tape to tightly secure it in place.

8. Now you're ready to set up your dry ice and start your fog tornado! Bring your tornado box to a clear, flat surface. Then, using your oven mitts, bring out the bag of dry ice and set it on a towel. Use your hammer to break off a few small pieces of dry ice.

   SAFETY NOTE: Carbon dioxide gas freezes and solidifies at a temperature well below zero. For this reason, it can only take a few seconds of exposure to your skin to give you frost burns, or even frostbite! Wear insulated gloves when trying this experiment, and don't touch the dry ice with your hands!

9. Fill your bowl with almost boiling water, then use your tongs to pick up a few small pieces of dry ice and place them in the bowl.

10. Set the tornado chamber over your bowl, and then place the fan over the small opening at the top of the box. Make sure the fan is facing upward, so the air will blow up towards the ceiling, not into the box. Turn on your fan, and watch your vortex spin!

WHAT'S HAPPENING?

Your tornado chamber pulls air upwards and outwards, as well as in from the slits in your box, causing the spiraling vortex you see inside. A tornado is formed in similar conditions, as warm moist air meets with an incoming cold front, pushing air upwards and condensing into towering cumulonimbus clouds. This movement, combined with rapidly changing winds, can pull air into a spiraling updraft. Whipping around the updraft, these winds can cause tornadoes that tear through the countryside!

Frosty the SNOW CAN

Have you ever walked outside on a cold winter morning and seen the ground covered with frost? How does this frost form? What is it made of? With this project, you'll create a frosty experiment at home using a tin can, some water, and a little ice. Bundle up and discover the physics of temperature, condensation, and crystallization.

MATERIALS NEEDED

A clean tin can

Scissors

Googly craft eyes

Construction paper

Glue

Crushed ice

Salt

Water

Magnifying glass

178

PROCEDURE

1. Empty your can and thoroughly clean it. Then use your scissors, googly eyes, construction paper, and glue to decorate your can to look like a snowman!

2. Fill your can halfway with crushed ice, and add 2 tablespoons of salt to the surface of the ice.

3. Pour just enough water into your can to cover the ice. Don't fill it too much; you just want to create a thin watery layer over your ice.

4. Set your can in a cool, dry place, and observe it over the next 30 minutes. It won't take long for crystals to begin forming. Once you see some crystal growth, inspect it through your magnifying glass. What kinds of crystal formations can you see?

5. After about 30 minutes, you should also see a nice, thick layer of frost form on the bottom of your can. Look at the frost through your magnifying glass. Do the structures of the crystals look different? Are they bigger or smaller than they were before?

WHAT'S HAPPENING?

When you add salt to a mix of ice and water, it lowers the melting point of the ice, causing it to melt even though the temperature is below freezing. With the water temperature below freezing, the water vapor in the air begins to cool and condense on the side of the can. Frost forms before your very eyes!

TAKE IT FURTHER

If you've got a microscope and slides at home, scrape some of the frost from the can onto a slide, and check it out under the microscope. You'll get an up-close look at the structure of crystal formations. This is how frost forms outside, too!

Cloud in a Bottle

Have you ever wondered how clouds form in the Earth's atmosphere? If you look up on a clear day, you might see small wisps of cirrus clouds in the sky. Within a few hours, these wisps might grow into long gray blankets of stratus clouds. Or perhaps they will billow into fluffy cumulus clouds! With this experiment, you'll not only learn how clouds form, you'll also create your very own cloud in a bottle. By harnessing the power of air pressure, you'll explore the physics of weather in your own backyard.

MATERIALS NEEDED

Empty, clear 2-liter bottle

Box cutter

Cork

Bicycle pump with ball-inflating needle

Rubbing alcohol

PROCEDURE

1. Remove all labels from your 2-liter bottle so that you can clearly see inside. Make sure the inside is clean and dry.

2. Use your box cutter to carefully cut your cork in half. Then remove the needle from the bicycle bump and push it through the top of the cork until it comes out of the bottom.

3. Pour 2 tablespoons of rubbing alcohol into the bottle and swirl it around about 5 or 6 times.

4. Take the cork and press it into the top of the 2-liter bottle so that the bottom of the cork is facing inside the bottle, and the outer end of the needle adapter is outside.

5. Connect the adapter to the bicycle pump, and give it about 5 or 6 pumps. Stop pumping air into the bottle when the pump becomes difficult to push.

6. Release the pressure valve on the bike pump, and quickly pull the cork out of the bottle!

WHAT'S HAPPENING?

When you pump air into the bottle, it increases the air pressure until it is greater inside the bottle than it is outside. This increased pressure heats up the molecules of air and alcohol vapor inside the bottle. When you release the pressure and remove the cork, this instantly drops the pressure in the bottle. The molecules quickly expand outside the bottle, where they cool and condense back into tiny droplets of vapor, forming particles of foggy clouds!

30

Convection Currents in the ATMOSPHERE

Have you ever watched a thunderstorm form? Big, billowing clouds appear, the sky starts turning dark, the rain starts pouring, and then suddenly you can see bright streaks across the sky and hear the crashing boom of thunder! How do these storms form in the atmosphere? With this experiment, you'll model the currents of air moving around our atmosphere and figure out how they interact to create super-charged thunderstorms!

20

MATERIALS NEEDED

1 cup measuring cup

Water

Red and blue food coloring

Ice tray

Large glass bowl

Small glass vial, vase, or test tube

10

PROCEDURE

1. Fill a measuring cup with water and add 5-6 drops of blue food coloring, or enough to create a dark blue water. Stir until thoroughly combined, then fill an ice tray with the blue water and put the tray in the freezer to make blue ice cubes.

2. Once the ice is frozen, fill a large bowl with cold tap water. Then, fill the small glass vial or test tube with hot tap water, and add 5 drops of red food coloring to the hot water to create a dark red solution.

3. Place a couple of ice cubes on one side of your bowl, near the edge.

4. Holding your finger or hand over the mouth of the glass vial, place the vial at the bottom of the bowl, on the opposite side from the ice cubes. Gently let go of the vial.

5. Monitor your bowl over the course of about 15 minutes as you see layers of convection currents begin forming in your bowl!

WHAT'S HAPPENING?

Convection currents occur in the atmosphere due to the different densities of hot and cold air currents. Warm air rises when it is faced with an approaching front of cold air. This rising warm air creates a lot of moisture, while the cold air condenses it into a foggy vapor, forming towering cumulonimbus clouds. A static charge can build due to the friction of rapidly moving air within the clouds, which is released as lightning.

DRIP

CHAPTER 14

DROP

EXPERIMENTS WITH BUBBLES

POP

Whatever FLOATS Your Boat

How does a ship, often made with heavy metals like steel, float on water? When we're in a body of water, why do we float when we lie on our backs, but sink if we curl into a ball? With this experiment, you'll explore the concepts of density and buoyancy as you take objects that would otherwise sink, and make them float.

MATERIALS NEEDED

Bowl

Water

5 assorted coins

3 small toys or figurines

Modeling clay

Paper towels

30

20

10

PROCEDURE

1. Fill a bowl with water and set it aside. Pick up your coins and toys, and, one by one, drop them into the bowl of water. Do they sink, or do they float? Why do you think some of your objects sink while others are floating around on the surface?

2. Take a brick of modeling clay and knead it with your hands until it is pliable enough to play with. Mold it into a large ball and drop it in your bowl. Does it sink?

3. Dry off your ball of clay, and mold it into a flat, wide oval. Curl up the sides to make the shape of a boat, with walls that are at least ½" high all around the outer edge.

4. Test it in your water to see if your boat floats. You may need to try different shapes and heights of the walls around the edges to prevent water from coming into your boat. Once you've got a floating boat, take it out, dry it off, and set it aside.

5. Now it's time to fill your boat! Place your small toys and coins on the boat, and then place your boat in the water! Are your objects now able to stay afloat on the clay?

WHAT'S HAPPENING?

When you put objects in water, they sink to the bottom if they are denser than the water and can't push enough of the water out of the way to float on top of it. When you flattened your clay in this experiment, however, the large pocket of air inside your boat decreased the density, allowing the same amount of weight to actually float on the water.

POKING Holes AND PLUGGING LEAKS

If you poked a hole into a bag filled with water, it would probably leak everywhere, causing a huge mess, right? With this experiment, you'll perform a cool science trick using polymers and surface tension to prove that you can poke several holes into a bag of water without allowing any water to leak out. Grab a bunch of sharpened pencils and get ready to surprise your friends with this cool scientific stunt.

MATERIALS NEEDED

Plastic sandwich bags

Pencils

Pencil sharpener

Water

PROCEDURE

1. Fill your sandwich bag ¾ of the way with water. Seal it shut, leaving a small pocket of air inside the bag.

2. Sharpen about 5 or 6 pencils and then set them aside.

3. One by one, pick up your pencils and stab them through your bag! Firmly press the point of the pencil into the bag, and keep pushing until it comes out through the other side. Don't push your pencil all the way through, though, or you may end up cleaning a giant mess instead of plugging leaks.

4. Repeat this step with all your pencils. Poke them through at different angles, and different distances. How many pencils can you push through your bag until it starts leaking?

5. Try this experiment with a variety of plastic bags. Will a thick freezer bag hold more pencils than a thinner storage bag? What about a plastic produce or grocery bag? Can you try this experiment with a plastic bottle filled with water?

WHAT'S HAPPENING?

Your plastic bag is made up of polymers: tiny molecules that are linked together in strong, flexible chains. When you poke the pencil through the bag, the polymers in the bag link around the pencil, creating a tight seal. At the same time, surface tension of the water causes the molecules to pull in towards each other, and away from the outside air. These two forces prevent water from spilling out, even when several pencils are stuck through the bag!

Make Bubbles with DRY ICE

Dry ice, also known as frozen carbon dioxide gas, is a fascinating material for curious scientists of all kinds. It causes foggy bubbles to ooze out of bowls and cups, and makes for a dramatic display. With this project, you'll explore the wonders of physics as you create a soapy film over your dry ice, trapping the billowing gases inside to create giant bubbles of fog.

MATERIALS NEEDED

Old T-shirt

Scissors

Insulated safety gloves or oven mitts

Hammer

Flathead screwdriver

Dry Ice

Medium-sized bowl with a rim

Small bowl

Dish soap

Tongs

SAFETY NOTE: Carbon dioxide gas freezes and solidifies at a temperature well below zero. For this reason, it can only take a few seconds of exposure to your skin to give you frost burns, or even frostbite. Wear insulated gloves when trying this experiment, and don't touch the dry ice with your hands!

PROCEDURE

1. Use your scissors to cut a long, thick strip of fabric from an old T-shirt. Set the strip aside and save the rest of the T-shirt for future crafts!

2. Put on your insulated gloves or oven mitts, then use your hammer and screwdriver to break off a few small chunks from your dry ice.

3. Fill a medium and small bowl halfway with water. In the small bowl, add a lot of dish soap to make a soapy bubble solution. In the medium-sized bowl, add a few chunks of your dry ice.

4. Watch the bubbling and popping of the dry ice as it fogs up and bubbles over your bowl!

5. Remove your gloves, then dip your finger into the bubble solution and rub it along the rim of the larger bowl. Keep doing this until it is evenly coated in your soap solution.

6. Take the thin strip of fabric and completely soak it in the bubble solution. Then pull the soapy strip slowly across the top of the medium-sized bowl to leave behind a layer of soapy film that will hold in the "foggy" gas of the dry ice. This part may take a few tries! If it doesn't work the first time, dip your shirt again, and keep trying.

7. Watch as the gases push up against the layer of film to create a giant, growing bubble.

WHAT'S HAPPENING?

Dry ice is the solid form of carbon dioxide, frozen to extremely cold temperatures. As it heats up, it goes straight from a solid to a gas in a process called sublimation. When you pulled your soap-soaked shirt across the rim of your bowl, you created a barrier to trap those gases. Because the gas is heavier than air, it takes longer for the gas to rise, which is why your bubble can get so large before popping and spilling foggy vapor everywhere.

Colorful BUBBLE ART

Bubbles are both wonderful and mysterious. These floating orbs have long captured children's imaginations and inspired them to play. This experiment gives you a new way to enjoy bubbles. Did you know that you can use them to make art? With this activity, you'll explore the science of surface tension as you blow billowing towers of bubbles and imprint their shapes onto paper to create your own masterpieces!

MATERIALS NEEDED

1 cup water

Medium-sized bowl

¼ cup dish soap

¼ cup baby shampoo

Glycerin (or light corn syrup)

Food coloring

Drinking straws

White paper

30

20

10

191

PROCEDURE

1. Pour 1 cup of water into a medium-sized bowl, then add ¼ cup of dish soap, ¼ cup of baby shampoo, and 6-8 drops of glycerin. Slowly stir to combine until the solution is thoroughly mixed.

2. Add 8-10 drops of food coloring to your bowl, and stir to combine. If you want to experiment with a variety of colors, place drops of different colors in a circular pattern around your bowl, and let the colors sit.

3. Take your straw and start blowing bubbles in your bowl! Rotate the bowl as you blow to create an even tower of bubbles. Keep blowing your bubbles until they rise well above your bowl and create a dome of bubbles.

4. Place your piece of paper directly on top of your bubbles, covering them. Lift your paper to see the pattern of colors the bubbles have left behind!

5. Repeat steps 3 and 4 until your paper is covered in bubble print. You can also place your paper in different places on your bubbles to cover different sections of paper!

6. Congratulations, you've just made your own bubble art! You can use this to make cards for friends, as a background for a mixed media artwork, or simply put it in a frame and proudly display it in your room!

WHAT'S HAPPENING?

Bubbles exhibit both the physics of surface tension and evaporation. Water molecules pull into themselves and away from air, creating a sphere. The soap and glycerin strengthen the spheres, and hold the water between two layers of soapy film, slowing the process of evaporation. As you blow your bubbles, the food coloring is carried up into the bubbles, and transfers both its color and the shape of the bubbles onto your paper!

Bouncing BUBBLES

Most kids have a lot of experience blowing bubbles with a little plastic wand. If you've ever tried blowing a huge bubble, however, you'll often find that they won't grow very large and will pop before you're done blowing it. With this experiment, you'll harness the power of surface tension to create a standard bubble mix for everyday play, and a super bubble mix that makes strong, long-lasting bubbles that can grow as tall as you!

MATERIALS NEEDED

1 cup water

Small Bowl

Dish soap

Glycerin (or light corn syrup)

Pipe cleaners

Large bottle of baby shampoo

Large bowl

Yarn

2 drinking straws

Scissors

Measuring cup

30

20

10

PROCEDURE

TIP: You can find glycerin at your local pharmacy, in the skin care aisle. It usually comes in a small clear bottle.

This experiment calls for two bubble recipes: a standard bubble mix, and a super bubble mix! Compare the results with both bubble mixes to see which yields bubbles that grow larger and last longer!

PART 1, STANDARD BUBBLE MIX:

1. Pour 1 cup of water into a small bowl. Add ¼ cup of dish soap and 6-8 drops of glycerin. Slowly stir to combine until the solution is thoroughly mixed.

2. Use your pipe cleaners to create a small bubble wand! Bend one pipe cleaner into a circle. Bend another pipe cleaner in half, and twist it over the bottom of the circle to create a wand stem.

3. Take your bubble mix outside, and blow your bubbles!

PART 2, SUPER BUBBLE MIX!

4. Pour 2 cups of baby shampoo, 2 ½ cups of water, ¾ cup of dish soap, and 2 tablespoons of glycerin into your large bowl. Slowly stir until the mixture is thoroughly combined, while making sure to keep the mixture free from frothy bubbles.

5. Hold your drinking straw up to your yarn, to measure one straw length. Repeat this step until you have measured 8 straw lengths of yarn. Then cut the yarn and set it to the side.

6. Thread your yarn through two drinking straws, then tie the yarn ends into a small knot to create a closed loop. Pull your straws to opposite sides of the loop until you have formed a wide rectangular shape. Set aside.

7. Use your pipe cleaners to create a variety of bubble wands! You can make a small circle with one pipe cleaner, or twist three together to create a larger circle. Experiment with a variety of shapes with your bubble wands.

8. Carry your bowl, pipe cleaner wands, and yarn wand outside. Completely submerge each of your wands into the bubble mix, then take them out and blow through them!

9. With the yarn and straws, pull them out of the bubble mix, and widen the yarn so it is in a wide rectangular shape. Hold it out to one side and spin around. You should see large bubbles blowing out of your straw wand! Experiment with large sweeping motions with your hands and your bubble wands, to create the largest bubbles you can. Spin around, pull the wands from the bowl, up over your head. See what motions yield the largest bubbles!

WHAT'S HAPPENING?

Soap and water are both made of molecules that tend to pull toward each other into a sphere. In water, this is called surface tension, as water molecules are more attracted to each other than any other material. The soap forms two layers around the water, a hydrophilic layer that bonds to the water, and a hydrophobic layer that bonds to air. The glycerin slows the process of evaporation, leading to stronger bubbles that last longer.

TAKE IT FURTHER

If you have a small plastic kiddie pool and a hula hoop, you can blow bubble tunnels you can stand inside of! Add 5 gallons of water, 3 bottles of baby shampoo, 5 cups of dish soap, and a bottle of glycerin to your kiddie pool. Stir the mixture to combine everything, and let it sit for at least 30 minutes. Then stand in the bubble juice inside the pool, place the hula hoop around your feet and slowly pull it up over your head.

CRACKLE

CHAPTER 15

CRACKLE

ADVENTURES IN ELECTRICITY

ZAP

Charming Snakes with STATIC ELECTRICITY

Snake charmers have the mystifying power to get slithering snakes to wind their way up from the ground as if they are dancing. With this experiment, you can charm your very own snake, without any risk of being bitten! All you need is some tissue paper, a marker, and a balloon, and you're ready to charm paper snakes with the power of static electricity!

MATERIALS NEEDED

Tissue paper
(used for gift wrapping)

Marker

Scissors

Balloon

Wool, hair, or something
to rub the balloon on

30

20

10

197

PROCEDURE

1. Lay out one large square of tissue paper, smoothing out the creases to make it as flat as possible.

2. Take your marker and, starting from the center of your paper, draw a spiral as big as you can make it to reach the edges of the paper. Your spiral snake's body should be approximately 1" wide.

3. Use your markers to decorate your tissue with any design you like. This is your own artistic creation, so feel free to get as creative as you like!

4. Take your scissors and cut along the curved lines until you have a tissue paper snake! Lay it flat in front of you.

5. Inflate your balloon until it's large and firm and then tie it. Then rub it all over your head to build up a static charge! If your hair doesn't build static, you can also rub it on a wool or fleece sweater, or even the carpet.

6. Once you've built a sufficient charge, place the balloon on the snake's head or tail. The snake will stick to your balloon, and you can drag it upwards. Congratulations, you've just charmed your snake with static electricity! Time to experiment: How high can you make your snake go? How long will your snake stick to your balloon? Can you move your snake from one balloon to another? If you place your charged balloon on a wall, will the snake remain attached?

WHAT'S HAPPENING?

Atoms are the building blocks of everything in the universe. They are primarily made of three particles: protons, electrons, and neutrons. Protons have a positive charge, electrons have a negative charge, and neutrons are neutral. When you rub your balloon on a head of hair or a sweater, the friction knocks electrons off the surface and onto your balloon! These negatively charged electrons are attracted to the positively charged protons on your tissue paper, which is why the tissue sticks to the balloon!

Electrified ALUMINUM CAN RACING

Static electricity can make the hairs on your head stand up, but did you know you can use it to make objects move? With this experiment, you'll use the crackling power of static electricity to move a can across your floor, without using your hands. All you'll need is a balloon, a head of hair, and an empty soda can, and you're ready for a static-powered aluminum can race!

MATERIALS NEEDED

Empty aluminum soda cans

Balloons

A head of hair, wool, or a fleece sweater

Flat surface

Masking tape

Measuring tape

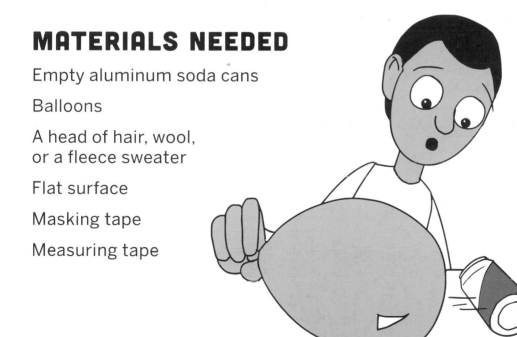

199

PROCEDURE

1. Lay your empty aluminum can so that it is resting on its side on your floor.

2. Blow up your balloon until it is fully inflated, and tie it. Then vigorously rub the balloon on your head, or on a wool or fleece sweater, to build a static charge. You'll know you've sufficiently charged your balloon if your hair sticks to it, or if you put it next to your arm and your arm hairs stand up.

3. Bring your balloon in front of the aluminum can so that it is almost touching it. Once your can starts rolling, slowly pull the balloon away from the can so it continues to roll toward the balloon across the floor!

4. Set up a race track on your floor by using your masking tape to mark off a "START" line. Then use your measuring tape to measure out 12" sections from the starting line. Use your masking tape to mark each 12" space until you've reached 4 or 5 feet away. Then, use your masking tape to mark a "FINISH" line!

5. Grab a friend and a couple of aluminum cans, and prepare to Get Ready, Get Set, Go! Charge your balloons by rubbing them on your head, or a sweater, and race your cans across the floor.

WHAT'S HAPPENING?

When you rub your balloon on your head or on a sweater, the motion knocks around parts of the atoms. This friction causes electrons to pull away from the surface, and onto your balloon, creating a negatively charged balloon. When you bring your balloon to the aluminum can, the electrons are attracted to the protons in the aluminum can. This attraction helps you pull the can toward your balloon.

THE ART OF WATER BENDING

Have you ever rubbed a balloon on your head, and noticed that your hair sticks to it? Have you gone down a slide at the playground, and gotten shocked as you jumped off? Both of these things can happen when you rub certain materials against each other, creating a buildup of static electricity. With this experiment, you'll harness the zap of a static charge to move atoms, create charges of electricity, and ultimately bend water.

MATERIALS NEEDED

Measuring cup or beaker

Water

Bowl

Balloon

Head of hair or wool or fleece sweater

PROCEDURE

1. Fill your cup or beaker with water, then set it aside next to your bowl.

2. Blow up your balloon until it is fully inflated and tie it. Then vigorously rub your balloon on your head or on a wool or fleece sweater to build up a charge of static electricity.

3. Hold your cup or beaker over your bowl and tilt it to start pouring water. Pour your water slowly, so that you have just a small stream of water pouring out.

4. Bring your charged balloon near your water. Don't let it touch the water, or your static charge will dissipate. Bring it just close enough to bend the water toward it.

5. Experiment with different rates of static charge. If you charge your balloon by rubbing it only three times, will it bend water at the same rate as if you rub the balloon several times? How much of an arc can you create with your water?

WHAT'S HAPPENING?

When you rub your balloon on a head of hair, or on a wool or fleece sweater, the friction knocks electrons off the surface, and onto your balloon. This causes your balloon to be negatively charged. These negatively charged electrons seek out positively charged protons to balance out the charges and create an equilibrium. When you bring your balloon close to the water, the electrons in the balloon try to attach to the protons in the water. This is why the water moves toward your balloon!

TAKE IT FURTHER

Can you bend other liquids with the power of static electricity? Will the density of a liquid change its ability to bend toward your balloon? Try this experiment with milk, oil, or vinegar, and see which liquids will bend the most, or not at all!

Flying Tinsel Cloud

We can feel a zing of electricity when we zoom down a park slide, or if we slide our feet across a floor and touch a metal doorknob. Static electricity can affect the world around us in many ways, but did you know that you could harness static electricity to make something fly? With this experiment, you'll use the power of static to create a floating ball of silver tinsel.

MATERIALS NEEDED

Long, thin strips of Mylar tinsel

Ruler

Scissors

24" long piece of ¾" PVC pipe

PROCEDURE

1. Take a few thin strips of Mylar tinsel and lay them on a flat surface in front of you, with the ends reaching the same points to create even lengths.

2. Take another piece of tinsel and tie a knot around one end of the grouped pieces of tinsel, so that they are all tied together in a tassel.

3. Use your ruler to measure six inches of tassel, and cut off the excess length. Then, trim the excess tinsel on the other side of the knot.

4. Now it's time to charge up your tinsel wand with static electricity! Take the PVC pipe, and vigorously rub it against the back of your head. If your hair doesn't build a static charge, you can try rubbing it against wool or fleece to build up that static charge.

5. Once you have a static charge built up, pick up your tinsel by one end, and hold it vertically over your wand. Drop it down, and watch what happens! Make sure you hold your PVC wand directly under the tinsel, and keep it away from your body so the tinsel doesn't fly towards you.

6. If your ball sticks to the wand, keep trying! Keep building a charge on your wand and drop the tinsel on to it, and it will bounce against the wand. You'll know you have it right when it bounces on the wand, and then immediately ricochets off, and starts flying in the air.

WHAT'S HAPPENING?

When you rub the PVC pipe in your hair, it knocks extra electrons onto the pipe, building a negative charge! Because the tinsel doesn't have a build-up of extra electrons, it is positively charged. Opposite charges attract, causing the tinsel to jump to the wand when you drop it from above. However, once it touches the wand, it too develops a negative charge. These like charges cause the tinsel to repel away from your wand and float through the air.

TAKE IT FURTHER

This experiment uses a PVC pipe, but you can try this trick with a balloon as well. Blow it up until it's fully inflated, build up a charge of static electricity, then drop your tinsel and watch it fly!

Make Your Own LEMON BATTERY

When we think of batteries, we usually imagine something we put into a remote or a game controller to keep it running. But what is a battery, and how does it work? With this experiment, you'll reveal the inner workings of a battery as you harness the power of electrical energy in an unexpected place: a lemon!

MATERIALS NEEDED

Wire cutter

Copper wire
(12- or 18-gauge)

Lemon

Safety pin

Red and black
alligator clip wires

Galvanized
(zinc-plated) nails

Voltmeter

PROCEDURE

1. Use your wire cutter to cut your copper wire into a 2" long piece and set it aside. If your wire has insulated coating over it, use wire strippers to cut and peel it off to expose the copper wire.

2. Roll your lemon on a flat surface, until it is soft and juicy. This breaks up the pockets inside the lemon, allowing juice to flow more freely on the inside.

3. Use your safety pin to poke a hole on top of your lemon, near one end. Wiggle the safety pin around a bit to widen the hole. Then press your copper wire into the hole, so that approximately 1" of copper wire is sticking into the lemon. Clip the red alligator clip firmly around the wire.

4. Take a galvanized nail and press it firmly into the lemon, until about 1" of it is sticking into the lemon. Clip the black alligator clip firmly around the nail.

5. Test for electricity! Take your voltmeter and match the colored wires to their corresponding alligator clips. Turn the voltmeter on to test for an electrical current, making sure that the voltmeter is set to DCV 20.

   When your voltmeter detects a current, you know that you've successfully turned a lemon into electric lemonade!

6. Now, stick two more galvanized nails next to the first, and two more copper wires next to the original copper. With more materials, can you yield a higher electrical output?

WHAT'S HAPPENING?

A battery requires three components for it to work properly: two electrodes and an electrolyte. The zinc and copper both act as electrodes, materials that will easily give up and accept electrons. This movement of electrons is what generates electricity. The lemon juice in this experiment serves as an electrolyte, providing a path for the extra electrons. The electrons head straight over to the copper wire, resulting in a movement of electricity that can be measured by the voltmeter.

Make Circuits with PLAY-DOH

We use electricity in almost every facet of our modern lives. From televisions to cell phones to computers to traffic lights, electricity is essential. We can experiment with electricity in our homes, but this can often require special materials and safety procedures. With this experiment, you can create your own electrical circuits with a safe and familiar material: Play-Doh.

MATERIALS NEEDED

Flour

½ cup sugar

3 tablespoons vegetable oil

½ cup distilled water

Measuring cup and a tablespoon

Bowl

Mixing spoon

Storage bag

AA battery pack with wires

Spade terminals (18-22 gauge)

Wire crimpers

Various colors of store-bought Play-Doh

LED lights

PROCEDURE

For this experiment, you'll make your own batch of insulated play dough and use it with your store-bought Play-Doh to light up your own circuits!

1. Mix 1 cup of flour, ½ cup sugar, and 3 tablespoons of vegetable oil into a large bowl.

2. Add ½ cup of distilled water to the bowl one splash at a time, allowing the water to be absorbed before adding more. Continue this process until your mixture has a dough-like consistency.

3. Knead the mixture with your hands to form a small ball of dough. Add water to soften, or flour to harden, until it has a Play-Doh-like consistency. Then put it in your freezer bag and seal it so the bag is airtight.

4. Now it's time to get your circuits ready! Remove the batteries from the battery pack. If the wires attached to your battery pack do not have a small amount of exposed wire at each end, use your wire strippers to cut and peel away a small part of the insulated coating.

5. Take the exposed end of the wire and run it through the spade terminal, until it is inside the small hollow groove near the base of the fork. Use your crimpers to tightly crimp the groove onto the wires. When you've finished crimping the spade terminals into each wire, place the batteries back in the pack.

6. Take two small pieces of store-bought Play-Doh, and roll them into a log shape. Stick the spade terminals into each one so that you have a red wire sticking into one piece of dough, and the black wire into the other.

SAFETY NOTE: Never touch the wires to the batteries, and try to keep them separated from each other. Never touch the posts of your LEDs to your battery terminals!

7. Place your separate dough pieces on a flat surface, ½" apart. Then take out one of your LEDs and place each leg into the dough! TIP: Look closely at the posts of the LED light. One post is slightly longer than the other. This larger end goes into the positive dough, the piece with the red wire sticking through it. The other end goes in the negative.

8. Build a bridge of LEDs with your Play-Doh! How many LEDs can you fit onto your Play-Doh?

9. Push the two pieces of dough together. What happens to the light when the dough is touching?

10. Take a small piece of your insulated dough, and roll it into a small log shape, the same length as your Play-Doh. Place it in the middle of the pieces, and then push them together. Now the Play-Doh is closer together, but not touching. You've made a wall of insulation between your dough. With everything touching, will your LEDs light up?

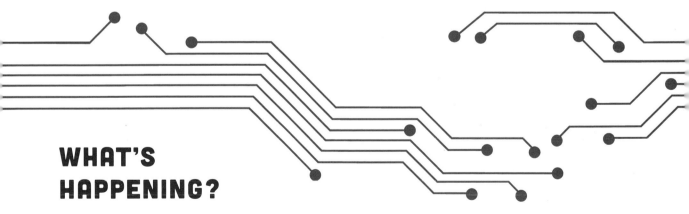

WHAT'S HAPPENING?

Play-Doh is a conductor; it easily allows electricity to run through it. It is high in salt, which acts as an electrolyte, allowing electrons to easily flow directly from the battery straight to your light source. Your insulated dough builds a wall between the electrons in the battery and your light. This allows you to build smaller and more intricate shapes with your dough, while also maintaining your electrical circuit!

REV

CHAPTER 16

ZOOM

THE SCIENCE OF SPEED

ROCKET

Vortex WATER RACES

How long does it take to empty a full 2-liter bottle of water? If you turn it upside down, air bubbles will have an interesting effect on the rate that the bottle empties. With this experiment, you'll explore the physics behind water and air pressure, and discover just what it takes to make a soda bottle empty faster. You'll even create a watery vortex tornado along the way!

MATERIALS NEEDED

2-liter bottle

Water

Paper and pen

Large bowl or kitchen sink

30

20

10

211

PROCEDURE

1. Remove all the labels from your bottle so you can clearly see inside.

2. Fill your 2-liter bottle completely with water. How long do you think it will take for you to dump it out? Write down your estimate.

3. Cover the mouth of the bottle with your hand to prevent any water from spilling out. Then set a timer and flip the bottle upside down over your bowl or sink so it's straight up and down.

4. Remove your hand and observe how long it takes for the water to drain completely. Don't shake the bottle or move it around, just let it sit there and drain the water out. Record how long it took.

5. Refill the bottle and repeats steps 3 and 4, but hold the bottle by the bottom, and swirl it in a circular motion. Swirl it about five or six times, until you get a vortex going! If you see a whirling water tornado, you know you're doing it right.

6. Record how long it takes for your water to drain out of your bottle.

7. Try it with a friend! Tell your friend you're going to have a race to see whose bottle will empty the fastest. While your friend is holding his bottle straight up and down, give yours a little twirl and surprise him with your tornado vortex victory!

WHAT'S HAPPENING?

When you flip the bottle upside down the first time, it takes a lot of energy to pour the water out. Air bubbles push into the bottle, with small amounts of water pouring out. When you give that bottle a spin, it creates an opening for the air, and the water gets pulled into a spinning vortex of centripetal force. This, combined with the force of gravity, causes the water to pour out at a faster rate than before!

BUILD A MARBLE RUN

Are you ready to think like an engineer with a need for speed? With this experiment, you'll flex your creativity as you create a twisting, turning, rollercoaster of a marble run. With trial and error, you can play with physics, mass, and gravity and race your way to the finish line with a marble run you can use again and again!

MATERIALS NEEDED

A wall or thick posterboard/cardboard

Toilet paper tubes

Paper towel tubes

Wrapping paper tubes

Duct tape

Scissors

Marble

Modeling clay (optional)

Paint (optional)

PROCEDURE

1. Use your scissors to cut all the paper tubes in half lengthwise, so that you have several long halves of paper tubing.

2. Begin with the highest part of your marble run. Cut a strip of duct tape that is as long as your paper tube, and press the tape into the inside edge of the paper tube. Place the tube high on your wall or mounting board at a slight downward angle, and press the tape firmly onto the wall to secure your tube in place.

3. Continue placing paper tubes one right after the other, so that each end is touching, and continue to angle your marble run downward. After placing three paper tubes on the wall, test your run with your marble to see if there are any adjustments you need to make to keep it running!

4. You may want to create twists and turns in your marble run so the ball can change directions as it goes. To do this, angle a tube so that it is facing the opposite direction slightly below the tube above it. This will allow your "switchback tube" to catch your marble and set it on a new course!

5. Once it's finished, take a step back and marvel at the engineering creativity you've shown! Then hold your marble at the top of your run, let it go, and watch it career to the bottom!

WHAT'S HAPPENING?

Your marble begins its run with potential energy that is determined by the weight of the ball, the path of travel, and the amount of gravity pulling on it. As the ball begins to roll, this potential energy changes to kinetic energy, which really gets things moving. As the acceleration increases, the smooth surface of the ball, coupled with the smooth surface of your tubes, allows it to retain that speed as it flies down the run.

Build a WATER ROCKET

People have been fascinated with flight for thousands of years. It is this curiosity that has led to the discovery of propulsion and the design of rockets that can launch into space. With this experiment, you'll explore the physics behind propulsion and rocketry while building your own supercharged water rocket that can fly high in the sky!

MATERIALS NEEDED

Box cutter

Wine cork

Bicycle pump with a needle adapter

Duct tape

Marker

Cardboard

Hot glue gun with glue

Empty 1-liter bottle

Paper plate

Scissors

Water

Bucket

PROCEDURE

1. Have an adult use the box cutter to cut the cork in half. Then remove the needle from the bicycle bump and push it through the top of the cork until it comes out of the bottom. Reattach the needle to the bicycle pump and set it aside.

2. Use the duct tape and marker to trace 3 half circles onto your cardboard. Cut them out, and trim them into the shape of rocket fins. Make sure there is one long flat side for easy attachment to your rocket, and one long curved side for aerodynamics.

3. Use hot glue to securely attach your fins to your bottle. Turn your bottle upside down, as the mouth of the bottle will be the bottom of your rocket. Place your fins near the bottom of the bottle, evenly spacing them around your bottle.

4. Cut out the inner circle of a paper plate, and discard the edges. Cut a straight line to the center of the circle, then bend the paper plate into a cone shape. Continue bending the cone until it fits over the rounded top of your rocket bottle. Use hot glue to secure it in place and trim off any excess material.

5. Now it's time to launch your rocket! Fill your bottle $1/3$ of the way with water, grab your small bucket, and head to a park. You'll want a lot of space, because your rocket is really going to fly!

6. Once you're in a wide-open space, secure the cork into the mouth of the bottle, insert the needle adapter of the bike pump into the hole you made in the cork, and place the rocket bottle in the bucket. The fins can brace against the top of the bucket, holding the rocket in place.

7. Start pumping air into your water rocket using the bike pump. You'll see bubbles in the water as the air is pushed through it. Continue pumping air until the rocket launches itself to the sky!

SAFETY NOTE: Never stand in front of the rocket, or point your rocket at anyone. These rockets launch at about 30 psi, which is a lot of pressure. These can injure someone if they're standing in the path of your rocket.

FUN TIP: Bring an extra 2-liter bottle of water, so you can keep launching your rocket over and over! The cork and the bottle will last for up to 50 launches, so you can keep trying to see how far your rocket can fly. You can also bring some extra duct tape to manage any leaks caused by the pressure from your launches.

WHAT'S HAPPENING?

When you pump air into your bottle, it increases the pressure inside. When this pressure reaches a point where no more air can be pumped into the bottle, the cork blows out and the water gets blasted out of the mouth. This action causes the equal and opposite reaction of your rocket launching up and outwards. This is a demonstration of Newton's Third Law of Motion. Scientists use this concept to build rockets that fly out into space!

TAKE IT FURTHER

Like the rockets that fly in space, your rocket has a nose cone and fins that help it fly faster and farther. These objects cut through the air and create a path for the air to fly around them, instead of pushing through it. This creates a more aerodynamic shape. You can experiment with this by removing the cone and fins. Will your rocket fly as far and high? Can you create an even more aerodynamic shape for better flight?

Fly High with a STOMP ROCKET

How do scientists and engineers design rockets and airplanes that are safe, balanced, fast, and durable? The answer can be found in physics, with a careful analysis of air pressure, thrust, and aerodynamics. With this experiment, you'll explore the physics of flight while stomping your way to rocket lift off. Harness the power of air pressure to explore flight and motion with your own backyard rocket launch!

MATERIALS NEEDED

Construction paper

24" of ½" PVC pipe

Duct tape

Marker

Paper plate

Cardboard

Scissors

7 feet of ¼" clear vinyl tubing
(½" outer diameter)

Empty and clean
2-liter bottle

PROCEDURE

1. Begin constructing your rocket body by wrapping your construction paper lengthwise around the PVC pipe. Tape the edges of the paper to create a paper tube, and remove it from the PVC pipe.

2. Using your marker, trace the outer edge of your duct tape roll onto your paper plate. Cut a straight line to the center of the circle, then bend the paper plate into a cone shape. Continue bending the cone until it fits on the top of your rocket. Use duct tape to secure it in place.

3. Use the duct tape and marker to trace 3 half circles onto your cardboard. Cut them out, and trim them into the shape of rocket fins. Make sure there is one long flat side for easy attachment to your rocket, and one long curved side for aerodynamics.

4. Bend the flat side so there is a ¼" flap along the flap side. Use tape to secure your fins to the rocket by taping the flap to the sides of your rocket.

5. Fit one end of your vinyl tubing into the mouth of the soda bottle. Wrap the end of the tube with several layers of duct tape to create an airtight seal around the mouth of the bottle.

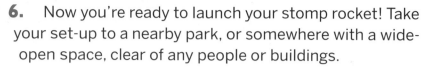

6. Now you're ready to launch your stomp rocket! Take your set-up to a nearby park, or somewhere with a wide-open space, clear of any people or buildings.

7. Place your bottle on the ground, and place the rocket onto the PVC pipe. Fit the PVC pipe over the vinyl tubing until the vinyl tubing touches the paper rocket.

8. Point your rocket away from yourself or anyone else. Then, using both feet, jump as high as you can and come crashing down onto your bottle. Watch as the pressure from your stomp launches your rocket high into the sky!

WHAT'S HAPPENING?

When you stomp on your bottle, the air inside is compressed into a smaller space, creating a high-pressure environment. This pressurized air moves through the hose, the PCV pipe, and into your rocket. Because the end of your rocket is closed, there's nowhere else for that air to move to, so it carries the rocket with it as it blasts forward! The aerodynamic shape of the nose cone and fins slice through the air, providing additional stability as it rockets upwards.

BALLOON Boat Races

You can make a makeshift boat out of a variety of light-weight materials, but did you know you can also make a boat that can move across a body of water? With this experiment, you'll harness Newton's laws of motion to propel a boat across the surface of water. All you need is a milk carton, a straw, and a balloon, and you'll be racing your way through the physics of rocket-powered boats!

MATERIALS NEEDED

½-gallon milk or juice carton
(with plastic screw cap)

Box cutter

Modeling clay

Drinking straw

Ruler

Scissors

Balloon

Rubber band

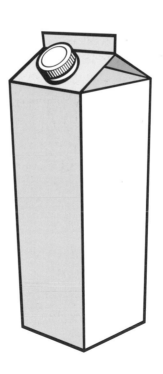

30

20

10

PROCEDURE

1. Remove and discard the cap of the milk carton and thoroughly clean the inside of the carton.

2. Place your carton on its side with the newly uncapped opening facing down. The back panel of the carton will be facing up. Use your box cutter to cut the entire back panel off of the milk carton so that it turns into a boat. (Your inflated balloon needs to fit inside.)

3. Take a large piece of modeling clay, and knead it until it is soft and flexible. Form a flat disc with the clay about the size of the mouth of the carton, and open a hole in the center, so the shape resembles a donut.

4. Insert the drinking straw into the clay, with 2" of the straw sticking out of one side, and the longer portion of the straw sticking out the other side. Seal the inside of the clay doughnut around the straw so that it forms a tight seal, with no cracks where water can get into the straw.

5. Push the long side of the straw into the mouth of the milk carton so that the short side is outside, and the long side is inside.

6. Measure approximately 3" of straw on the inside of the milk carton, and use your scissors to cut away the excess. Pull the straw back out of the mouth of the milk carton.

7. Stretch your balloon until it becomes elastic and flexible. Then pull the neck of the balloon over the long end of your straw and use a rubber band to secure the balloon in place.

8. Push the balloon and the straw back into the mouth of the milk jug. Press the clay around the outside of the mouth to form a watertight seal.

9. Use your mouth to inflate your balloon through the straw, and then pinch the straw to keep any air from escaping.

10. Bring your balloon boat to your desired launching site, and place the boat in the water so that the short end of the straw is completely submerged. Release your hand from the straw, allowing the air to escape the balloon. Stand back, and watch your boat take off!

WHAT'S HAPPENING?

Newton's Third Law of Motion states that for every action, there is an equal and opposite reaction, and that's exactly what powers your boat! When you inflate your balloon, it holds a potential energy that is converted to kinetic energy as the air is released. The force of the air leaving the balloon propels your boat forward. Your boat is buoyant because it displaces more water than the carton weighs, allowing it to float on the surface of the water.

TAKE IT FURTHER

You can construct a balloon-powered boat from a variety of resources. With this experiment, you used a milk carton, but you can also use a piece of Styrofoam, a pie tin, an aluminum roasting pan, other materials. As long as it floats, you can cut a hole for your straw, and you're good to go! Get creative with your designs, and hold a balloon boat race with your friends!

MENTOS and Diet Soda ROCKET CAR

Mentos and Diet Soda are fun ingredients for scientists in training because they react together in a fizzing explosion of bubbles! Did you know this high-powered energy can also be used to fuel backyard rockets? With this experiment, you'll build your own car that you can race using this exciting combo of ingredients. All you need is some cardboard, candy, and soda, and with a little help from the great Isaac Newton, you'll be well on your way to racing with rocket-powered chemistry!

MATERIALS NEEDED

2-liter bottle of diet soda	Pliers
Ruler	Paper
Cardboard	Soup can
Glue gun	A pushpin
Wire cutters	4 flat thumbtacks
2 metal coat hangers	1 package of Mentos
2 ballpoint pens	

PROCEDURE

1. First, make a three-sided box to fit over your soda bottle. Using your ruler, measure the length and width of your soda bottle. With these dimensions, draw three rectangles (one for each side of the soda bottle) on your cardboard. Cut them out, and use hot glue to attach them to three sides of your soda bottle.

2. Use your wire cutters to cut two straight pieces of coat hanger that are 2" longer than your pens.

3. Using your pliers if necessary, remove the ink cartridges from your pens. Then, poke one of your coat hanger ends through each pen to pop out the cap on the end. Discard the caps, and set the coat hangers and the empty pen barrels to the side. These will be your wheel axles.

4. Use the soup can to trace 8 circles onto your cardboard for the wheels, then cut them out. Use your hot glue gun to glue pairs of cardboard wheels together. Now you have 4 solid wheels for your car! Use your pushpin to make a hole in the center of each wheel, and widen the hole until you can just see through it.

5. Using the pliers, bend the end of one of your coat hanger pieces into a right angle, about ¾" from the end. Slide one wheel onto the piece of hanger, and hot glue the bent end against the side of the wheel.

6. Poke the remaining end of the hanger piece through an empty pen barrel. Slide another wheel onto the hanger against the pen, bend the metal hanger, and glue the bent end of the hanger onto the wheel. Repeat this process with the remaining hanger piece, pen barrel, and wheels.

TIP: Once your glue is dry, you should be able to spin the wheels. If they stick, check to make sure there isn't any glue on the pens. If there is, simply remove it, and your wheel should spin freely.

7. Use hot glue to secure one of the pen axles to the bottom $1/3$ of your soda bottle, so that each wheel is sticking out the sides of the bottom. Secure the other axle on the top $1/3$ of the soda bottle in the same fashion. You've built the bottom of your rocket car!

8. Cut some small strips of cardboard to glue front to back over the center of your axles. This will help to secure the axles while you're racing your car over bumpy terrain.

9. Fit your three-sided box over the soda bottle. On the bottom edge, poke two thumbtacks through the cardboard, one in front of the front wheels, and one behind the back wheels. Do the same on the other side. Use hot glue to secure them in place, and stretch a rubber band to connect the front thumbtack and rear thumbtack together on each side. This will hold the top in place. Tip: You can also glue the top on to the bottle.

10. Now you're ready to race! Carry your full rocket bottle outside. Head to an empty parking lot or road. Make sure you have an open space, as these rockets can travel up to 40 feet!

11. Roll a piece of paper into a long tube and tape one end. Drop your Mentos inside the tube. Then slowly open the soda bottle, and lift it so the mouth is facing upward. Quickly drop the Mentos inside, set the car on its wheels before the reaction begins, and watch it take off!

WHAT'S HAPPENING?

Mentos contains a lot of small dents on the surface of the candy shell. When you drop them into the soda, carbon dioxide bubbles quickly form on these dents and build on each other until so much pressure builds, it explodes out of the back of the soda bottle! This in turn pushes your soda bottle forward, as every action creates an equal and opposite reaction. Thus, it is Newton's Third Law of Motion that launches your rocket, propelled by pressurized soda down the street!

CRUSH

CRUMPLE

OBJECTS UNDER PRESSURE

 # SHRIEK

Air Pressure CAN CRUSHING

To crush an empty aluminum can, you might use your hands, squeezing it until it crushes between your palms. Or you might stomp on it, crunching down with your feet. With this experiment, you'll crush cans without having to use any part of your body. You'll use the power of air pressure to crush your cans with almost no effort of your own All you'll need is some heat, some ice, and about 1,000 pounds of air pressure!

MATERIALS NEEDED

Large bowl

Ice

Empty soda can

1 tablespoon of water

Stove top or camp stove

Safety goggles

Tongs

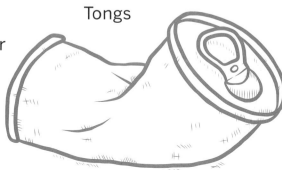

PROCEDURE

1. Fill your bowl with ice water and set it aside. You'll want at least one ice cube tray of ice in there to make an ice water bath.

2. Fill your empty soda can with about 1 tablespoon of water. Place your soda can in the center of a pan on your stove. Put on your safety goggles, grab your tongs, and observe.

3. Heat your can until the water starts boiling. You will know this is happening when you start to see steam escaping from the top of your can. You might also hear little popping sounds as air bubbles begin to pop inside.

4. Using your tongs, quickly and carefully pick up the can, immediately bring it over the bowl, and, in the same motion, turn it upside down and plunge it into the ice water bath. Observe what happens to your can.

WHAT'S HAPPENING?

Earth's atmosphere starts way up in space and presses down on us with a weight of about 14.7 pounds per square inch! We don't feel this because it's pressing down from all sides, as well as pushing out from within our bodies. In this experiment, most of the air in your can expands and escapes as you boil the water inside it. When you put the can in ice water, the air remaining inside cools off and compresses. With no air pushing outward to resist atmospheric pressure, the intense pressure of the atmosphere is able to easily crush your can.

WATER on the RISE

Earth's atmosphere protects us from the sun's harmful rays and burns meteors as they hurl toward the planet, causing the "shooting star" effect we might see on a clear night. The atmosphere has a lot of other fascinating properties too, including the fact that it presses on us at a constant rate! We don't feel this pressure because the pressure inside our bodies equalizes it. With this experiment, you'll be able to harness the power of air pressure, fire, and water to make water rise!

MATERIALS NEEDED

Birthday candle

Lighter (ask for adult supervision)

Plate

Water

Tall narrow jar (glass, vase, or flask)

Food coloring (optional)

PROCEDURE

1. Have an adult help you light your candle. Drip a few drops of candle wax onto the center of your plate. Quickly blow out the candle and stick it in the wax.

2. Pour a bit of water on the plate, making sure that the base of the candle is covered in water.

3. Have an adult help you relight your candle.

4. Quickly and carefully cover your candle with the jar! Make sure the bottom of the jar is submerged in the water and not pressing on the candle.

5. Stand back and observe the effects of the atmosphere on your water!

WHAT'S HAPPENING?

When you light the candle and cover it with the jar, it rapidly heats the air around it, causing it to expand and escape. This creates a space similar to a vacuum. The air pressure outside of the jar is no longer equal to the pressure inside the jar, so it pushes the water into the jar to make up for the difference, creating an equilibrium.

TAKE IT FURTHER

Try this experiment with several candles. Does it change the rate at which the water rises? You can also experiment with different temperatures of water. Will ice cold water rise at the same rate as room temperature water—or even hot water?

Dry-Ice SCREAMING Pennies

Time to have some fun with the billowing fog clouds created by dry ice! In this experiment, you'll take this frozen carbon dioxide gas and boil it using only a penny. You'll explore the physics behind changing phases of matter and the powerful pressures of the atmosphere. Get your gloves, grab some spare change, and get ready to make your coins scream.

MATERIALS NEEDED

Dry ice

Oven mitts

Hammer

Flathead screwdriver

Tongs

Gloves

Large plastic storage container

Pennies and other assorted coins

Metal spoon

PROCEDURE

This experiment works best outside on a flat surface. Don't try this on the kitchen table!

1. Use your oven mitts to pick up your dry ice and set on a flat surface. Use your hammer and screwdriver to break off a few small chunks from your dry ice.

2. Use your tongs to pick up a few pieces of dry ice and set them into the plastic storage container. Once you've got a few pieces in there, it's time to put on your gloves and get to experimenting.

   SAFTEY TIP: Carbon dioxide gas freezes and solidifies at a temperature well below zero. For this reason, it can only take a few seconds of exposure to your skin to give you frost burns, or even frostbite. Wear gloves when trying this experiment, and don't touch the dry ice with your hands!

3. Pick a flat piece of dry ice, and set a penny on it so that the penny is lying flat. Use your gloved finger to press down on the penny for approximately 1-2 seconds. Do you hear the shrieking sounds it makes? Lift your hand away from the penny after 2 seconds, so the freezing temperatures don't hurt you!

4. Now, try the same thing with a variety of coins. Try a nickel, a quarter, or any other metal coins you have. Do you get the same result?

5. Try pressing your spoon against a chunk of dry ice. You can even try your tongs, and your screwdriver! Try placing a variety of materials against the dry ice. Do plastics, cloths, or rubber yield the same results?

WHAT'S HAPPENING?

Dry ice is a solid form of carbon dioxide, frozen to extremely cold temperatures. When you press the coin into the dry ice, the metal conducts heat into the ice, causing it to boil away into a gas. This gas boils away at such a high pressure and speed against the coin that it makes a screaming noise as it rushes past! As the coin loses heat, it no longer "boils" the ice, and the sound stops.

Pressure-Powered SUBMARINES

How does a submarine go from diving through the ocean deep, to coming up to the ocean's surface? What forces are at work to allow these vessels to operate so seamlessly? With this experiment, you'll explore the forces of extreme pressure and density as you make your own Cartesian diver and witness the science of submarine diving in the deep sea.

MATERIALS NEEDED

2-liter soda bottle

Water

Medicine dropper

Modeling clay

Glass

PROCEDURE

1. Remove all the labels from your clean 2-liter bottle so that you can clearly see inside.

2. Fill your bottle all the way with water. Fill your medicine dropper halfway with water from the bottle.

3. Take a pea-sized amount of modeling clay and affix it to the bottom of your medicine dropper, forming a watertight seal.

4. Take your glass and fill it with water. Drop the medicine dropper in to test its buoyancy. If it floats, you're good to go! If it sinks, remove a small amount of clay until it floats on the surface.

5. Once your dropper floats, it's time to drop it into the bottle. Place it inside, and then screw on the cap until it is tightly sealed.

6. Place your hands near the middle of the bottle and give it a hard squeeze. If you see the air begin to rise in your dropper, keep squeezing. Soon, your dropper will start plummeting to the bottom of your bottle.

7. This may take a few tries to get just right. Keep squeezing the bottle, and letting go, until you see the air begin to rise in the dropper.

WHAT'S HAPPENING?

When you squeeze the water bottle, it forces water into the medicine dropper, and causes the small pocket of air inside to condense into a smaller space. The molecules within the air become more tightly packed together, which increases the air's density and makes it sink to the bottom of the bottle. When you stop squeezing the bottle, the air expands into the dropper again, causing it to rise to the surface.

EGG IN A BOTTLE

Can you push an egg into a bottle without using your hands? With this experiment, you'll harness the power of physics to do the seemingly impossible! Using air pressure, a little bit of heat, and a hard-boiled egg, you'll set an egg in the mouth of your bottle and watch it get pushed inside by an invisible force!

MATERIALS NEEDED

Medium-sized hard-boiled egg

A tall jar with the mouth just slightly larger than your egg

Matches

Paper

PROCEDURE

TIP! Wood matches work well for this experiment. If you're using paper matches, try rolling a 2" piece of paper, lighting it with the match, and dropping it into your jar.

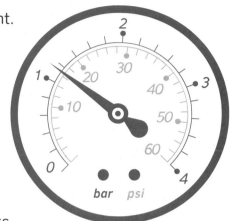

1. Boil your eggs in a rolling boil for approximately 15 minutes. Make sure the egg is hard boiled, as a soft-boiled egg may break in your jar.

2. Carefully peel the hard-boiled egg so the surface is smooth and round, without cracks or dents.

3. Bring your boiled egg and your jar over to a clear flat surface. Have an adult help light two matches, and drop them into the bottom of your jar.

4. Quickly place your hard-boiled egg over the mouth of the jar, and step back.

5. Observe what happens to the flame in the jar, and the egg at the top of the jar.

WHAT'S HAPPENING?

The weight of Earth's atmosphere is constantly pressing down at a rate of about 14.7 pounds per square inch. When you place the egg on the bottle, the air is pressing down on the egg, but also pushing up from within the bottle. When you light the match, it causes some of the air in the bottle to heat and expand, escaping out of the top. Now the pressure is greater outside the bottle than inside, causing that weight to press down on the egg, and push it into the bottle.

SPARKLE

CHAPTER 18

AND

THE MYSTERIES OF SPACE

SHINE

Dropping METEORS on the MOON

When you look at the moon, what is the first thing you see? You might notice how bright it is as it reflects the sun's light down to you. Or, you might notice the "face" of the moon, the dark spots that pepper the landscape and give it the look of "The Man in the Moon." Those dark marks are craters left from meteors that blasted the moon's surface. With this experiment, you'll be powering meteors and changing the face of an artificial moonscape.

MATERIALS NEEDED

Large shallow pan

Play sand

Bead

Pom-pom craft ball

Large marble

Play-Doh

Ruler

Pen and paper

PROCEDURE

1. Fill your shallow pan with play sand to a depth of approximately 1 ½". Shake the pan until the sand falls into a flat, even layer. This will act as the surface of the moon.

2. Lay the bead, pom-pom ball, and marble out in front of you in a line. Use your Play-Doh to make a ball that is larger than your large marble. These will act as your meteors!

3. Use your pen and paper to make a data table. Draw it so that it has 4 rows and 4 columns. On the left side, name each row with one of your balls (bead, pom-pom, marble, Play-Doh). Label the top of your columns with "Prediction", 12", 18", and 24".

4. Make predictions on which balls will make the largest impact craters in your sand, and write your predictions down in your first column using words like: "largest", "second largest", and "smallest".

5. Now it's time to drop your meteors! Start with the smallest object, and hold it at a height of 12" over your sand. Let go of the ball and see if the impact forms a crater. If it does, measure the depth and width and record those numbers on your table.

6. Take turns dropping each object (or "meteor") from the same height, and measuring the depth of the crater, making sure to mark the measurements on your table.

7. Follow the same steps, but drop your balls from 18" and 24". Do the craters change shape and size if you drop them from greater heights?

WHAT'S HAPPENING?

If you've seen a shooting star, you've observed a meteor burning through Earth's protective atmosphere before it hits the ground. If it hits, the impact causes even the smallest meteorites to eject several tons of dirt from the surface of the Earth. Scientists study patterns in the layers of ejected dirt and rock to determine the size of the meteorite.

Chocolate Cookie MOON PHASES

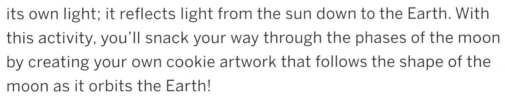

When you look up in the night sky, the first thing you see might be the bright moon shining down from above. The moon, however, doesn't shine with its own light; it reflects light from the sun down to the Earth. With this activity, you'll snack your way through the phases of the moon by creating your own cookie artwork that follows the shape of the moon as it orbits the Earth!

MATERIALS NEEDED

Paper plate

Blue, green, white, and brown paint

8 chocolate sandwich cookies

Butter knife

PROCEDURE

1. Prepare your Earth by painting a representation of it onto a paper plate. Get creative as you paint oceans, land, and clouds swirling around through the atmosphere.

2. Open all 8 of your cookies, trying to leave all of the white frosting on one half. Save the top half of one cookie for your new moon and prepare to create edible models of all of the other phases.

3. Using the image provided here as a reference, use your butter knife to sculpt out the phases of the moon on each of your cookies. The eight moon phases you need to create are:

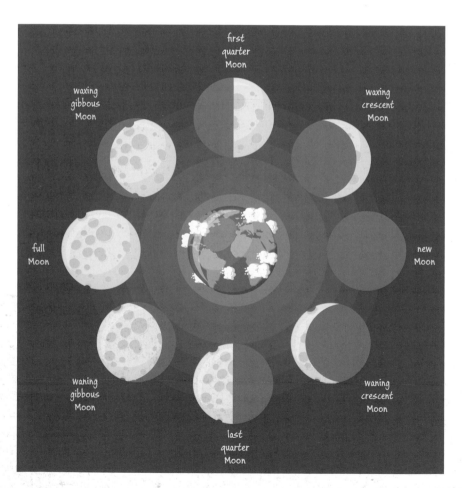

NEW MOON
chocolate top of cookie

FULL MOON
half of cookie with all of the white filling

HALF MOONS
First quarter (right half frosted), Third quarter (left half frosted)

CRESCENT MOON
Waxing (right crescent), and Waning (left crescent)

GIBBOUS MOON
Waxing (right almost full), and Waning (left almost full)

4. Finally, place your moons in position around the Earth. If you were to think of the Earth as a clock, place the New Moon at 3:00. Then, working in a clockwise motion around the Earth, evenly space your moons with the Waning Crescent, Last Quarter, Waning Gibbous, and then the Full Moon, on the opposite end at 9:00.

5. Continuing in a clockwise motion, place the Waxing Gibbous, the First Quarter, and Waxing Crescent to complete your phases of the moon model.

    Congratulations! You're about to snack your way through the phases of the moon! Grab some cookies and have fun eating your way to a new moon!

WHAT'S HAPPENING?

The moon shines with light that is reflected from the sun. As it orbits the Earth, the light we can see changes based on its position relative to the Earth and the sun. During a new moon, it is positioned between the Earth and the sun, and all light is reflected back towards the sun. During a full moon, the Earth is between the moon and the sun and a full face of reflected light can be seen on the moon's surface. The slivers of light that we see in the changing phases are due to the moon's moving in and out of these two positions as it orbits the Earth.

TAKE IT FURTHER

You can also demonstrate the phases of the moon at home using a lamp with the shade taken off, a foam ball, a pencil, and a dark room. Poke the pencil into the ball and hold it up at arm's length above your head. Turn on the light, and while holding your moon in space, slowly spin around in a circle. You'll begin to see the light reflected off your moon, in the same shapes you made with your cookies!

Build a WORKING TELESCOPE

Have you ever looked up in awe at the dazzling array of stars and the glowing moon of the night sky? For thousands of years, people have been fascinated by celestial objects and have been working on ways to see them more clearly. With this experiment, you'll follow in the footsteps of Galileo and some of the greatest scientists in history when you work to create your own working telescope. Get ready to see the starry sky in a whole new way.

MATERIALS NEEDED

Concave and convex lenses
(with the same focal length if possible)

Wrapping paper tube

Ruler

Marker

Scissors

Paint or decorative tissue

Electrical tape

244

PROCEDURE

1. Start with a set of concave and convex lenses (purchase them at a hobby shop or online). A concave lens is flat on one side and curved on the other. A convex lens is curved on both sides.

2. Identify the focal length of your lenses. This experiment works well with a focal length of 50 cm, but other lengths work as well.

3. Make the paper tube as long as the focal length of your lenses. Measure and mark the distance on the tube and cut off any extra.

4. Decorate your telescope! You can use paint or decorative tissue paper to create a beautiful telescope for your explorations in astronomy.

5. Once you've finished decorating, it's time to put your lenses in place. Look through your convex lens, to see which side allows you to magnify. Place your lens in that same position on one end of your tube, and use electrical tape to secure it in place.

6. Look through the concave lens to determine which side allows you to see clearly. Place the concave lens in that same position on the other end of your tube, and secure it in place with electrical tape.

7. Test your telescope outside. Look through the end with the concave lens, and see what comes into focus. Flip your eyepiece lens if needed.

8. Take your telescope outside on a clear night, and use it to explore the surface of the moon!

WHAT'S HAPPENING?

You constructed a refracting telescope. The convex lenses pull in a lot of light, magnifying an image so we can see it. This light refracts (bends) around the lens until it reaches the focal point, where it condenses to form an image. The concave lens in the eyepiece gathers light from the focal point and projects magnified light waves onto the back of your eye, where it can be interpreted by your brain as an image.

Flashlight CONSTELLATIONS

Step outside on a clear night and you may see a sky flooded with stars. Since the beginning of civilization, people have been tracking the stars, noting their position in relation to other stars, and creating stories about them. However, if the sky is filled with clouds, or too much illumination from the lights in your city, you might not be able to see many stars. With this project, you'll ensure that you always have a front row seat to the incredible constellations above.

MATERIALS NEEDED

Pencil

Flashlight

Black cardstock

Pushpin

Constellation guide

Electrical tape

Scissors

PROCEDURE

1. Using your pencil, trace the outer edge of your flashlight onto some cardstock. You'll trace the top of the flashlight, where the light shines out, to create small discs that will fit inside.

2. Cut at least five of these "constellation circles" from the cardstock and set them aside.

3. Refer to the constellation guide here or online, and draw some of your favorite constellations on each disk. Connect the lines with your pencil, and make sure to draw dots where the stars would fit in the constellation.

4. Use the pushpin to push holes where the stars would be. Then use your pencil to push through the holes to widen them.

5. Trim the circles as needed so they will fit on the end of your flashlight. Be careful not to over trim.

6. Use electrical tape to secure your disks onto your flashlight and to block any light from escaping the outer edges.

7. Turn off the lights in the room and switch on your flashlight to see the constellations flash across your wall!

WHAT'S HAPPENING?

You can easily replicate the shapes of your favorite constellations! The holes you punch in the cardstock become the stars that shine on the wall and form dazzling celestial displays.

Additional Resources

THE SCIENTIFIC MOM:
(AUTHOR'S BLOG, SCIENCE EXPERIMENTS, ENGINEERING PROJECTS, AND MORE)

thescientificmom.com

SCIENCE EXPERIMENTS, SCIENCE FAIR IDEAS, AND MORE

sciencebob.com

homesciencetools.com

sciencebuddies.org

ENGINEERING AND DESIGN

makezine.com

LEARNING CHALLENGES AND ONLINE TUTORIALS

diy.org

**IN-DEPTH, EASY-TO-UNDERSTAND EXPLANATIONS
IN SCIENCE, HISTORY, AND MORE!**

thecrashcourse.com

ANIMATED LESSONS IN SCIENCE THROUGH TED EDUCATION

ed.ted.com

INDEX

A

Absorption
Water Bead Osmosis, 111
Acids and bases
The Big Squeeze: Intestines at
Work, 85
Cabbage-Water Chemistry, 58
Color-Changing Explosions, 122
Fabric Art with Acids and Bases,
60
Fizzing Volcanoes, 120
It's a Gas! The Magic of CO2, 126
Air currents
Convection Currents in the
Atmosphere, 182
Air pressure
Air Pressure Can Crushing, 228
Balloon Boat Races, 221
Egg in a Bottle, 236
Fly High with a Stomp Rocket, 218
Pressure-Powered Submarines,
234
Water on the Rise, 230
Animals
Fossil Footprints, 34
Ants
The Ants Go Marching, 38
Apples
Rotten Apple Chemistry, 51

B

Battery
Make Your Own Lemon Battery,
205
Birds
Darwin's Finches, 36
Bubbles
Bouncing Bubbles, 193
Colorful Bubble Art, 191
Make Bubbles with Dry Ice, 189

C

Candy
Candy Chromatography, 67
Floating Candy Letters, 72
Inside a Gobstopper, 70
Lightning Life Savers, 76
Marshmallow Animals Gone Wild,
74

Carbon
Grow a Giant Carbon Snake, 128
Centrifugal force
Vortex Water Races, 211
Chromatography
Autumn Leaf Mash-Up, 18
Candy Chromatography, 67
Clouds
Cloud in a Bottle, 180
Compass
Make Your Own Bottle-Cork
Compass, 170
Compost
Make Your Own Compost, 23
Constellations
Flashlight Constellations, 246
Crystals
Crystal Snowflake Ornaments, 157
Frosty the Snow Can, 178
Grow Your Own Crystal Garden,
155
Molten Magma Rock Candy, 146
Salt Crystal Tower, 149

D

Density
Liquid Rainbow Tower, 62
Sinking and Floating Eggs, 64
Whatever Floats Your Boat, 185
Digestive system
The Big Squeeze: Intestines at
Work, 85
Eat Your Cake and Digest It Too, 83
DNA (deoxyribonucleic acid)
Squishing Out Strawberry DNA, 48

E

Earthquakes
Jell-O Earthquake Engineering, 135
Play-Doh Plate Tectonics, 142
Eggs
Disappearing Eggshells, 54
Egg in a Bottle, 236
Sinking and Floating Eggs, 64
Electrical circuit
Make Circuits with Play-Doh, 207
Erosion
Cookie Continents and Ocean
Erosion, 139

Evaporation
Colorful Bubble Art, 191
Exothermic reactions
Elephant Toothpaste, 124
Eyes
Make a Frozen Lens, 94

F

Flotation
Balloon Boat Races, 221
Whatever Floats Your Boat, 185
Fossils
Fossil Footprints, 34
Frost
Frosty the Snow Can, 178
Fruits
Make Your Own Lemon Battery,
205
Rotten Apple Chemistry, 51

G

Gas
Bubbling Wonders Lava Lamp, 118
Dry-Ice Screaming Pennies, 232
Elephant Toothpaste, 124
Erupting Soda Geysers, 116
Fizzing Volcanoes, 120
Grow a Giant Carbon Snake, 128
It's a Gas! The Magic of CO2, 126
Make Bubbles with Dry Ice, 189
Mentos and Diet Soda Rocket
Car, 224
Geology
Metamorphic Candy Bars: The
Science of the Squish, 151
Molten Magma Rock Candy, 146
Play-Doh Plate Tectonics, 142
Sample the Earth's Core, 137
Seven-Layer Sedimentary
Crackers, 153
Gravity
Build a Marble Run, 213

H

Hand
Make a Skeleton Hand, 81
Heart
A Bloody-Good Heart Pump, 88
Crafting the Human Heart, 90

I

Ice
    Frosty the Snow Can, 178
Insects
    The Ants Go Marching, 38
    Bright Lights and Buggy Nights, 40
    Build an Insect Hotel, 44
Iron
    Magnetic Cereal: Where's the Iron?, 164

L

Leaves
    Autumn Leaf Mash-Up, 18
    Make a Leaf Skeleton, 25
Light. See also Sunlight
    Lightning Life Savers, 76
Liquids
    The Art of Water Bending, 201
    It's Alive: The Properties of Slime, 107
    Liquid Rainbow Tower, 62
Lung
    Build a Balloon Lung, 79

M

Magnets
    Dancing Magnetic Slime, 162
    Magnetic Cereal: Where's the Iron?, 164
    The Magnet-Powered Pendulum, 166
    Make Your Own Bottle-Cork Compass, 170
    Recording Magnetic Fields, 168
Mass
    Build a Marble Run, 213
Meteors
    Dropping Meteors on the Moon, 239
Microbes
    Finding Life in a Drop of Water, 42
Milk
    A Dish of Dancing Rainbows, 56
Moon
    Chocolate Cookie Moon Phases, 241
    Dropping Meteors on the Moon, 239

N

Newton's laws
    Balloon Boat Races, 221
    Build a Water Rocket, 215
    Mentos and Diet Soda Rocket Car, 224
Non-Newtonian fluids
    It's Alive: The Properties of Slime, 107

Nucleation
    Salt Crystal Tower, 149

O

Oceans
    Cookie Continents and Ocean Erosion, 139
Osmosis
    Water Bead Osmosis, 111

P

Pendulum
    The Magnet-Powered Pendulum, 166
Pheromones
    The Ants Go Marching, 38
Plants
    Color-Changing Carnations, 28
    Make a Leaf Skeleton, 25
    May the Best Soil Win, 21
Polymers
    Bouncing Polymer Putty, 109
    Dancing Magnetic Slime, 162
    Poking Holes and Plugging Leaks, 187
    The Science of Stickiness, 113
    Snow in Summer, 173
    Water Bead Osmosis, 111

R

Rockets
    Build a Water Rocket, 215
    Fly High with a Stomp Rocket, 218
Rocks. See Geology

S

Sight
    Colorblind Taste Test, 96
    Make a Frozen Lens, 94
Smell
    The Scent Detective Game, 102
    Smell It, Don't Tell It, 104
Soil
    Make Your Own Compost, 23
    May the Best Soil Win, 21
Sound
    Sound Gun Science, 98
Stalagmites
    Hair-Raising Jell-O Stalagmites, 159
Stars
    Flashlight Constellations, 246
Static electricity
    The Art of Water Bending, 201
    Charming Snakes with Static Electricity, 197
    Electrified Aluminum Can Racing, 199

    Flying Tinsel Cloud, 203
    Hair-Raising Jell-O Stalagmites, 159
Submarines
    Pressure-Powered Submarines, 234
Sunlight
    Build a Pinhole Solar Eclipse Viewer, 11
    Build a Solar Oven, 8
    Building a Spectrometer, 14
    Solar Photography, 6
    Solar-Powered Pinwheels, 4
Surface tension
    Bouncing Bubbles, 193
    Bubbling Wonders Lava Lamp, 118
    Colorful Bubble Art, 191
    A Dish of Dancing Rainbows, 56
    Poking Holes and Plugging Leaks, 187

T

Taste
    Colorblind Taste Test, 96
Tectonic plates
    Play-Doh Plate Tectonics, 142
Telescope
    Build a Working Telescope, 244
Thunderstorms
    Convection Currents in the Atmosphere, 182
Tornadoes
    Build a Tornado Chamber, 175
Touch
    The Ouch Sensitivity Test, 100

V

Volcano
    Build an Underwater Volcano, 132

W

Water
    The Art of Water Bending, 201
    Bouncing Bubbles, 193
    Bubbling Wonders Lava Lamp, 118
    Build a Water Filter with Sand and Rocks, 30
    Colorful Bubble Art, 191
    Frosty the Snow Can, 178
    Poking Holes and Plugging Leaks, 187
    Vortex Water Races, 211
    Water on the Rise, 230
    Whatever Floats Your Boat, 185